KEY A1

Pocket Teaching Guide

Von Jeremy Taylor

Cornelsen

Key A1 Pocket Teaching Guide

Verfasser
Jeremy Taylor, Brno

Beratende Mitarbeit
Dietlind Unger, Leipzig

Außenredaktion
Janan Barksdale, Berlin

Verlagsredaktion
Martin Maier

Projektleitung
Murdo MacPhail

Illustration
Christian Bartz, Berlin (Kopiervorlagen); Bettina Kumpe, Braunschweig (Seite 5)

Titelbild
Image courtesy of TFL (London Transport)

Umschlaggestaltung
Klein & Halm Grafikdesign, Berlin

Layout und technische Umsetzung
zweiband.media, Berlin

www.cornelsen.de

1. Auflage, 1. Druck 2010

Alle Drucke dieser Auflage sind inhaltlich unverändert und können im Unterricht nebeneinander verwendet werden.

Druck: Druckhaus Berlin-Mitte GmbH

ISBN 978-3-06-020103-7

Inhalt gedruckt auf säurefreiem Papier aus nachhaltiger Forstwirtschaft.

Contents

Symbols used in this Pocket Teaching Guide

pairwork activities

group activities

1.13 CD and track number

answer key or suggested answers

photocopiable material

Introduction

Welcome to KEY!

KEY is a new concept. With KEY we want to make it easy for teachers to teach great lessons, and also to make it easy for learners to make fantastic progress and enjoy learning English - and all with a minimum of stress for everyone.

Our 'take and teach' format means you can just pick up the book and teach. All the activities are clearly presented on the page with simple instructions. Each double page spread is one lesson, and each lesson has the right balance of speaking, listening, reading, writing, grammar and vocabulary. You can be sure each lesson contains a variety of interesting practice opportunities for your learners.

One central element of KEY is that in each lesson, your students will talk about themselves, their lives, their opinions, their experience. The English they learn is exactly the English they need to talk about what is most important to them. KEY really is a fully personalized English course.

Of course this Teaching Guide gives you the answers to the activities, but that's not all - you'll also find lots of extra ideas for your lessons.

KEY concept

KEY A1 has 12 units that cover stimulating themes. The clear structure matches the learning needs of adult learners at A1 level.

- Each unit has four related parts - or lessons.
- Lessons A and B introduce the topic and provide basic practice of the new language with a variety of activities.
- Lesson C offers more practice opportunities on the theme, and consolidates the grammar and vocabulary in new and interesting ways.
- Lesson D has lots of quick grammar and vocabulary exercises, together with reading and listening exercises for important skills practice. It's also a great way of measuring progress, and you can use it as handy homework for your students.

In addition to interesting lessons, KEY also offers you and your students regular Journal pages. These colourful, authentic materials have been chosen because they are interesting, relevant and memorable - your students will want to read them and talk about them, even out of class. In fact, we don't think you will be able to stop yourself!

Here are some of the advantages KEY offers you and your students:

- Lots of variety, so students are always interested.
- A range of activity types to suit all sorts of learners.
- KEY verbs, to help students develop their vocabulary and fluency quickly.
- Short and manageable activities that give everybody a sense of achievement.
- Lots of authentic materials from newspapers, magazines and conversations so your students practise real English in real situations.
- Hundreds of oral pairwork activities so that your students use the English they've just learnt immediately.
- A strong focus on personalized activities, so students can talk about themselves, their lives and their opinions.
- Grammar activities related to real contexts, so the new grammar structures are easy to understand and apply.

We hope you all enjoy teaching with KEY!

The KEY authors & editorial team

Teaching tips

In the next few pages we offer a few teaching tips that you may find useful. Teachers with very little teaching experience might like to read these pages carefully. Those teachers with more experience may also like to have a look as there is always something new to learn.

An A1 class is likely to contain a mix of real beginners, those who have no English whatsoever, and false beginners, those who claim to be beginners, but in fact can get by on holiday with their limited English, though it may be littered with errors. To make things easier for teachers of such classes we have provided some typical phrases for instructions on the inside front cover of the coursebook. These are both in English and in German and will help your real beginners feel less intimidated by this 'strange new language'.

If you have a large number of real beginners then clearly you will have to take things slowly at first. They need a lot of repetition and plenty of support and praise for their first tentative steps. In the opening units there are a lot of international words, for example, words that the students are likely to have seen when travelling around an environment such as an airport. This will help boost their confidence. KEY A1 can be used with real beginners, but it is important not to miss out Part C of each unit as this will help the students consolidate the structures and languages that were covered in the first two parts. If your class consists of false beginners, then you should still start at the beginning but you will be able to move at a slightly faster pace and, if necessary, leave Part C as optional for your students.

One of the big problems for you as a teacher is how to deal with students of different abilities. For this reason, the first topic for the teaching tips is how to deal with heterogeneous classes.

Getting the most from ... mixed-ability classes

No test that is given to students before joining a new language class will divide the students perfectly – you will not have 25 clones, all with the same level of listening, reading, speaking and writing skills. There is a wide range of activities in KEY, and you will find that some students find some tasks easy, while others struggle. While the students are working on an exercise, doing a mill and match, for example, you have the opportunity to move around and help the ones who need more help. The Teaching Guide also offers a number of extension exercises, which the faster students can do while the weaker ones are finishing the main exercise. Finally, the photocopiables sometimes incorporate a section for slightly higher level students.

For those of you working with some real beginners, you may like to get some of your stronger students to help them. Often this can help both students. Try to rotate the 'helpers' so that no one feels used.

Top ten tips for a successful mixed-ability class

1. When arranging groups, try to get a mix of strong and weak students in each group.
2. At times, get the stronger students to help the weaker students.
3. Praise your weaker students for their contributions as their confidence is likely to be shaky.
4. If your weaker students need some extra help, allow the other students to continue with another exercise while you sort out a particular problem. Don't feel that all the students have to be doing the same thing at the same time.
5. While monitoring, try to have a chat with the weaker students to build up their confidence. Don't forget the stronger students may like to be stretched so have a chat with them at a slightly higher level than is normal in the class.
6. Encourage the group to work as a team in their struggle to learn English. This will make the group more cohesive and make things easier for you (and them).
7. When giving homework, consider giving different homework to different students to cope with their different abilities.
8. Enjoy the variety of activities that every unit of KEY offers. If your weaker students find something a little tough, they can be sure that something easier will be just around the corner.
9. If stronger students finish before the others, encourage them to look at Part C of the unit, or they can read the journal material.
10. If students are much too strong or too weak for the group, have a word with the director of studies about the possibility of moving them to a higher or lower group where they will feel more comfortable. This will also be better for the others in the group who won't feel discouraged by someone much better than they are - or have to feel sorry for someone who is much weaker than they are.

Getting the most from ... speaking tasks

In KEY A1 there are many different kinds of speaking activities as this is the skill that most students want to improve. You will find:

- **Pairwork - problem solving:** Definitely two heads are better than one when it comes to solving a problem.
- **Pairwork - exchanging views:** The KEY exercises are designed so that the students can exchange views on a wide variety of topics - and also use the target grammar and vocabulary frequently and painlessly.

- **Pairwork – answer checking:** Once students have completed an exercise it makes a lot of sense to check their answers with their partner. If there are any discrepancies, they have time to look again.
- **Group work – prioritizing exercises:** There are many exercises in KEY in which the students have to prioritize something. This could be the order in which they organize a holiday or the most important qualities for friendship. The important thing about such exercises is that there is no correct answer: the students themselves will decide the order, and the answer that they come up with is of secondary importance compared to the discussion that went on to produce the answer.
- **Group work – brainstorming:** This is a great opportunity for your students to pool their resources and come up with some creative ideas. It might be a meal for a visitor from another country, it could be things to do on a wet Saturday afternoon, but encourage them to be as creative as possible.
- **Group work – sharing responses:** In many exercises, once the exercise has been done in pairs, the students then share these responses within a group. Many students find this recycling of their ideas very useful as it builds up their confidence.

Top ten tips for a good speaking activity

1. Make sure the students know what to do before they start the speaking activity. Rather than repeating the instructions twice, you may like to get one of your students to reiterate the instructions.
2. Don't ask the question *Do you understand what to do?* as it is unlikely a student who doesn't understand what to do will have the confidence to say so.
3. You may like to model the interaction before the students all start talking. This is particularly useful for an activity like 'find someone who' with which some students may not be familiar.
4. Make sure that the students are talking (a lot) more than you.
5. If there is an activity in which the whole class is involved, e. g. asking each other for information, feel free to join in. The students will benefit from your model answers, and you can be part of the buzz of a successful class.
6. In general, encourage fluency rather than accuracy. After the activity you may like to look at some of the errors being made, particularly if it involved the target structure.
7. When you talk to your students, talk as naturally as possible. Ask *Have you ever been to Brazil?* as though you genuinely want to know the answer, rather than the question being just another example of the present perfect.
8. Encourage your students to talk to a variety of partners. Practice makes perfect, and if they can ask (and answer) their questions ten times, then it will be better than asking and answering just once.

9 Many of the exercises in KEY get the students to talk about their own experiences and opinions. This allows the students to find out more about each other and keeps an activity fresh.

10 Make sure you conclude the activity before the students run out of ideas. Though originally from the world of show business, the rule 'stop while the audience wants more' is good advice in the classroom as well. A lively and fun discussion may run for 3-4 minutes but if you try to let it run for 10 minutes then you will get some bored students. Given the great variety in KEY, your students can be sure that it won't be long before they are given the opportunity to have another enthusiastic discussion!

Getting the most from ... listening tasks

Listening tasks are vital for your students to hear a great variety of English. BBC English is not the only English in the world and in KEY your students will be exposed to a wide variety of accents and English spoken by people of different ages.

In KEY you will find lots of listening comprehension exercises and they are always supported with an activity for the students to do while listening. It is always a good idea to discuss the recording before you play it, by saying, for example: *We're going to hear an interview between a television producer and two people who want to be on a reality TV show. What kind of questions do you think he will ask?* If you do this kind of pre-listening task, your students will be better prepared for when they hear the dialogue. If your students look puzzled at the end, offer to play it again. Before you do, get them to discuss the answers that they did get.

Many of the recordings in KEY have more than one exercise. This will mean your students will hear the recording more than once. The more often they hear it, the easier it is for them to understand it.

Top ten tips for a good listening exercise

1 Get the CD ready to play before the class begins.
2 Introduce the topic of the listening to whet your students' appetite for the subject.
3 Give the students time to read the exercise before you play the recording.
4 Expect to play the recording more than once.
5 Teach your students the phrase: *Could you play that again, please?*
6 Sit still and listen to the recording with the students. Don't distract them.
7 If your students are struggling, stop the recording a few times to give them time to complete the exercise.

8 Another way to help struggling students is to allow them to look at the transcripts – though try not to encourage this for everyone.
9 If the acoustics are poor in the classroom, get your students to come closer to the CD player.
10 After the recording, get your students to discuss the answers to the exercise in pairs or small groups.

Getting the most from ... reading tasks

Reading is a very important skill and there is plenty of reading practice throughout the book. However you won't find many long passages as reading a passage for more than a few minutes does not give rise to a lively classroom atmosphere that your students will enjoy.

One problem that some students have with reading in a foreign language is that they want to understand every word. They sit with a difficult text and stop every sentence to look up the meaning of a word (or three) that they don't know, or perhaps just to check that they have understood the word correctly. It is a good idea to encourage your students to look at the context in which a word appears and have a good guess at the meaning. Secondly, do they really need to know the word to understand the text? Often it is better for them to keep reading and not worry about every word that is unfamiliar.

Reading is a great way to introduce new vocabulary and structures to students and the more they read, the more frequently they will come across these new words, and the better their English will become.

KEY is quite special in that there are regular journal pages which your students can read just for pleasure.

Getting the most from ... the Journals

The Journals are a special part of KEY and it is entirely up to you (and your students) how you use the material found there. One possibility is to simply say *Enjoy!* and let your students browse through the journal when they have a free moment and look at the articles that they find intrinsically interesting. This is particularly useful if you have a heterogeneous class and some students need some extra 'stretching'. The journals are the perfect answer to this. They contain language and structures that may be new to the students, but the combination of strong visuals and intrinsic interest should mean that your students will want to get as much as they can from the articles.

Another way to use the Journals (especially Journal I and II) is to bridge the gap between semesters. During this time away from weekly lessons, some students feel their English start slipping as they don't get the opportunity to practise. The Journals are an ideal way for your students to keep their English alive during those lonely weeks between English courses.

Having said all that, we are also aware that some teachers (and some students) might want to use some of the Journal material in class and prefer a little more guidance in doing so. In this Teaching Guide you will find some tips as to how you might want to exploit the journals with your students.

Top ten tips for working with the Journal pages

1. After students have read a story, do a dictation with one part of it. You can either make a small number of changes as you dictate while the students try to remember the original, or you ask them to work in pairs to recall what the next part was.
2. Ask students to complete a tic-tac-toe grid and put nine key words or phrases from the text in the nine squares. Then they compare what they chose and see who has the same, and discuss any differences. They can use the grids to play tic-tac-toe where they can only 'win the square' if they make a correct sentence with the word.
3. Ask pairs to summarize the page in one line of not more than 15 words. Again, ask pairs to compare and vote on the best.
4. Tell students to read the text, then test one another on what they remember. One takes the role of questioner and the other tries to answer from memory.
5. Give pairs five minutes to re-read the page and make five collections of words from it. Examples could be: verbs, adjectives, numbers, words ending with s, prepositions. Then, using the collections, see how much of the text they can recall.
6. All the journal pages have strong visuals. You can ask pairs to concentrate on the visuals for one minute, then you ask a number of testing questions, e.g. *How many red objects were there in the picture? Was the sky cloudy or not? Was the man wearing jeans or shorts?* You could then ask pairs to do the same.
7. Pairs read the whole journal and then vote on the most interesting/unusual/shocking/memorable/colourful page.
8. Give pairs a list of grammar items that occurred in recent units to look for, e.g. uncountable nouns, irregular plurals, expressions with key verbs, past tenses or modal verbs.

9 Pairs imagine what happened immediately before and after each picture and discuss their stories.
10 Pairs rewrite one part of one page of the journal as a dialogue, then read the dialogue to the class.

Getting the most from ... working with photos

KEY is full of some excellent photos and these can be used in many different ways. Often they help to focus the students' attention on a particular subject: holidays, food, emotions, etc. There are also many exercises which involve the students looking at the photos – which is good for your visual learners. A fun game to play with your students is to choose a photo from KEY at random. The students can ask questions to find out what is on the photo, but you can only answer with *yes* or *no*. Once you have played it, you can get your students to play the same game in groups.

The photos also allow you to stretch the stronger students in a heterogeneous group, for example by extending vocabulary: *So, Beate, what's the name of the thing that the man is wearing to stop his trousers falling down? (I think it is a belt.)*

Getting the most from ... the photocopiables

There are a total of 24 photocopiables in the KEY package which complement the exercises in the coursebook. You will find a wide range of activities, and the photocopiables themselves can be used in many different ways. Some groups of students might enjoy the anarchic approach of running around the classroom, trying to match up various parts of a sentence. Other groups may prefer to do the same exercise sitting around a table in quiet discussion with their fellow students. You know your students best, so you decide how best to exploit the material that is available. It is a good idea to familiarize yourself with the photocopiables before using them. Read through the advice on how to use the material in the Teaching Guide and decide what will work best for you.

Below is a list of all the photocopiables so that you have a convenient checklist.

Photocopiable	Good for ...	Your notes
1 Unit 1 Part B Detective at the airport	Airport vocabulary, numbers	
2 Unit 1 Part C Countries & capitals	Country & capital names	

3 Unit 2 Part A I get up at ... And you?	Simple present	
4 Unit 2 Part B Is there?/Are there?	*There is/there are* in question form	
5 Unit 3 Part A Where to go?	Holiday vocabulary, *likes + -ing*	
6 Unit 3 Part C This, that, these, those	*This/that, these/those*, nationalities & adjectives	
7 Unit 4 Part A Find someone who ...	Simple present	
8 Unit 4 Part B Does ... ?	Questions with *does*	
9 Unit 5 Part A Secret Diaries	Simple past, Days of the week	
10 Unit 5 Part B William's story	Support for exercise 6 (Sequencing)	
11 Unit 6 Part A All you need is ...	*Need*	
12 Unit 6 Part B Big, bigger, biggest	Comparatives & superlatives	
13 Unit 7 Part C Are you good at ...?	*Good/fantastic/brilliant at doing sth*	
14 Unit 7 Part B Negative adjectives	***un**lucky, **dis**honest*, etc.	
15 Unit 8 Part A Can you ...?	*Can/can't*	
16 Unit 8 Part B Have you got ...?	*to have got*	
17 Unit 9 Part A Which do you prefer?	*to prefer*	
18 Unit 9 Part C Bob's bedroom	Prepositions of place	
19 Unit 10 Part A Ask Janet	Giving advice	

20 Unit 10 Part B Imperatives	Imperatives	
21 Unit 11 Part A Going to ...	*Going to ...*	
22 Unit 11 Part B Too ...	*Too* + adjective	
23 Unit 12 Part A Write a note ...	Writing practice	
24 Unit 12 Part B Showing what you feel	Talking about emotions	

Getting the most from ... classroom set ups

You may not have a choice in this as the tables may be screwed to the floor. But, if you do have a choice, you may like to arrange your students in small groups around a table so that they can carry out pairwork and group work easily. At times you may like get your students to sit in a large horseshoe so that everyone can see everyone else. Of course, the set up that you use will depend on the facilities available but in KEY there are a variety of different activities and sometimes moving the furniture around will make the task more effective.

Even if your furniture is fixed, there is no good reason why your students should work with the same people every minute of every lesson. It is refreshing for them to get up, move around and then work with a new partner or group.

Top ten tips for a mixing up groups

1 Tell the group: *Everyone who is wearing a ring (or wearing something blue or wearing black shoes), change places!*
2 Get your students to arrange themselves in order of their birthdays (not date of birth!).
3 Get your students to arrange themselves alphabetically.
4 Write famous couples on separate pieces of paper. Hand out the pieces. The students then have to find their partner: *Excuse me, are you Delilah? (Yes, Samson!)* They now have a new person to work with.
5 Write questions and answers on separate pieces of paper and hand them out. The students then have to find their partner: *Do you know when the last people walked on the moon? (Yes, it was 1972!)* They now have a new person to work with.

6 Write numbers on separate pieces of paper and hand them out. The students then have to find their partner: *Excuse me, is your number 390? (No, sorry. I have 319.)* They keep going until they find the person with the same number.
7 If your students are sitting in a horseshoe, simply move one person from one end of the horseshoe, to the other. In that way, everyone has a new partner.
8 Write A, B and C on a number of pieces of paper. The students take one each and then form three groups of As, Bs and Cs. (Clearly, if you want more groups, you can add more letters.)
9 Get your students to arrange themselves according to their height.
10 Get your students to sit next to someone that they don't know very well.

Getting the most from ... feedback sessions

In KEY there are many exercises in which your students work in groups. It is not possible to monitor all groups all the time but a good feedback session will allow you to discover whether the students have completed the task, whether there are any outstanding problems that need to be addressed and whether the group needs more practice of the target structure or whether they are ready to move on.

Top ten tips for a good feedback session

1 Make sure that all your students listen to other groups during a feedback session.
2 Ask some checking questions to make sure everyone is listening. (For example: *Which of Sabine's recipes did you like most?*)
3 You don't have to get feedback from every group, after every activity.
4 Make sure that everyone gets a chance to give some feedback, but don't put pressure on the shy or weaker students.
5 Show genuine interest in their answers: *You went to Kenya on holiday? Wow, what was it like?*
6 Try to avoid giving your students the opportunity to answer with just *yes* or *no*. Compare: *Did you have a good time in Majorca?* with *Tell me some of the things you saw in Majorca.*
7 Don't always take the answer from your best students. Try to give the others a chance.
8 If a query comes up in the feedback session, you may want to deal with it straight away. If you think it might take longer, ask the student to make a note of the query so that you can discuss it later.

9 If someone asks you a question and you don't know the answer, admit it, and compliment them on asking such a good question. Make a note of it and get back to the student next lesson.
10 When someone gives you an answer, don't always tell them if it is right or wrong, but ask the opinion of the other students. This makes sure that the students listen to each other's answers, and also enables a healthy debate about the answer.

Getting the most from ... the Homestudy sections

At the end of each unit there is the Homestudy section (Part D). Here you will find excellent consolidation material, which the students can do after each Part (A, B and C) or all together at the end of the unit. Or, if they are too busy, there is no obligation for them to do it at all (though we don't want to encourage this!).

The students can self correct as there is an answer key at the back of the book. While the section is intended for homestudy, there is no reason why you can't use some of the exercises in your classes. Especially in heterogeneous classes, you could have the stronger students do, for example, one of the writing exercises while the others are busy with something else. Similarly, weaker students could benefit from doing some of Part D while working together with a partner, rather than on their own back at home.

However you choose to use it, the Homestudy section is a useful resource which gives your students extra practice of the structures and language covered in earlier parts of the unit.

Getting the most from ... the Portfolio pages

You'll notice as you flip through the book, that Parts C and D of Unit 12 are different than in the rest of the book. In Part C there is a pinboard with 'Can you ...?' questions and in Part D you'll find the Portfolio pages.

The pinboard in Part C is closely connected to the tasks stipulated by the can-do statements in Part D (see below). The photographs and notes on the pinboard have been carefully selected to reflect the unit contents and are supported by the three sets of 'can you?' questions (colour-coded to match the three semesters of the book). The visuals and questions together can be used as a springboard for revision and discussion, either at the end of each unit or at the end of a semester, and offer even those teachers who choose not to use the Portfolio pages a creative and informal way to revise much of the material covered in the book.

Part D offers a more formalized way of dealing with (and covering) can-do statements. The portfolio pages can be used to keep track of students' progress and to check whether they have reached the learning targets (unit aims).The set-up is easy. Each unit has three can-do statements that reflect that units' contents and aims, both thematically and grammatically. Should the students feel they need more help with a particular area, they can look at the pages in the Units or Grammar section indicated in the table. Underneath each unit's can-do statements, there is a task that invites the students to actually show what they can do – using visuals either on the pinboard or in the units.

Learning strategies on the right of each chart offer some additional help to the learner, but are not actually related to the units' contents or aims.

Ideally, the students should refer to the Portfolio pages upon completion of each unit. They can look at the can-do statements and do the practical task. If the students require further help, they can follow the links to the parts of the book where they can find out more about a particular language area.

It is useful for the students if the Portfolio pages can be looked at in class time. This will allow your students to ask you for help – if such help is needed. Once they have filled in the Portfolio pages for a couple of units, they may feel confident enough to be able to fill it in themselves in their own time.

1

At the end of unit 1 your students should:

- be able to use the simple present of the verb *to be: I am, you are, she/he/it is.*
- have practised introductions and greetings.
- have learnt vocabulary connected with airports and travel.
- have practised saying simple numbers and the letters of the alphabet.
- have talked about cities, countries and nationalities.

A And you?

coursebook pages 10–11

1 In this first exercise, your students have to match the English words with where they came from originally. Since most of the words are the same or similar in German, this warmer should help students see how many English words they already know. Have them start with the easier word pairs (i. e., *kindergarten* and *rucksack* from Germany) and they should be able to get them all. Get them to help each other and you can jump in if they have problems.

Germany	kindergarten, rucksack
Czech Republic	pistol, robot
France	restaurant, film
Italy	studio, piano
Africa	banana, chimpanzee
India	shampoo, cashmere

2 **1.2** Your students will hear three simple dialogues on meeting and greeting new people and old acquaintances, and can read the dialogues at the same time. (Though if you have a class of false beginners, you could also have them listen with their books closed the first time around.)

In the second part of the exercise, the object is to match the photos with the dialogues.

1 C 2 B 3 A

3 All of the phrases in this matching exercise come from the dialogues students have just heard and read. If they need more help, they can look at the dialogues again.

1 C 2 F 3 D 4 A 5 G 6 B 7 E 8 H

4 A speaking exercise. Your students may be a little nervous so you might want to model the conversations with them. (Also, if necessary, draw their attention to the box on page 10 and the differences between Mr, Mrs and Ms.) Most of your students will probably be from the same country so it makes more sense to say the town or village you are from rather than everyone saying they are from Germany or Austria.

5 1.3 A nice simple listening for your students with a manageable task. Make sure the students understand that they need to choose between two words in the first dialogue and fill in the missing words in the second.

A Dublin, US, LA

B Hamburg, Bristol, the UK

6 Some more conversation practice. Encourage your students to move around the class and practise the dialogue with as many people as possible. You should join in as well, paying particular attention to anyone who seems to lack confidence.

7 The students just need to write two questions (e. g. *Where are you from? How are you?*). They should then either ask their partner the questions, or stand up and move around, asking as many people as possible.

Extension activity: It is not easy to learn all the names of the students on the first evening but you can make a game of it. *So, you're Angela from Stuttgart? (No, I'm Beate from Reutlingen.) Oh, I'm sorry. OK, now you're Sebastian from Ulm ... (No, I'm Steffen from Leipzig! This is Sebastian from Ulm.)* Your students will hopefully realize that you are playing a game but by correcting you they will be practising the structures of the first lesson.

There is a short text by Lisa Lubin on the right. Your students may read it and get curious about the journals (where there are quite a few articles by her), but it is not a formal part of the lesson.

B Where are you?

coursebook pages 12–13

1 A simple matching exercise for phrases connected with airports. Your students are likely to have seen these phrases many times at airports. There is also some help from the photographs.

Photos in anticlockwise direction, starting at top left:
car park – duty free – information desk – passport control –
departure lounge – meeting point – hotel reservations – coffee shop

2 A memory test for your students, which you could get them to do in pairs. They both look at the pictures and phrases for 20 seconds. Then student A closes the book and tries to remember as many of the places as possible. (Student B can tick them off as they are mentioned.) Then student B can look at the page for 20 seconds while student A ticks off the items. Which student in the class has the best memory?

3 **1.4** Listening exercise. Here is a simple dialogue between a travel rep and a tourist at an airport. The students can also read the dialogue in the book. If you have some false beginners whose English is better than the others, you might ask them to close their books and just listen to the dialogue.

First name: Ashleigh   Country: UK/Scotland   City: Aberdeen

In the second part of the exercise, students get a chance to practise spelling. Some of your students may know the names of the letters in English, others may not. It may be worthwhile going through them with your students while paying particular attention to the vowels. In any case, spell a few countries or names for them to model the activity, before having them work in pairs.

4 Making questions. Have the students look at the grammar box on the verb *to be* before doing this exercise and encourage them to use the contracted form, i. e. *What's your name?* It sounds much more natural. When they give their answers, your false beginners will probably know the short answer forms *(Yes, I am. No, I'm not.)* but don't expect this of them at this stage. A simple *yes* or *no* is fine.

1 's   2 's   3 're   4 Are   5 are

5 **1.5** Listening comprehension. The students simply have to listen for and write in the places in an airport that they looked at on the previous page.

1 coffee shop   2 information desk   3 meeting point   4 car park

You may like to give your students a bit more time to complete the second part of the exercise. Have your stronger students correct the false statements.

1 False. He's at the *information desk*.
2 False. Sandra is in the coffee shop. (*Harry* is in the car park.)
3 False. She's with *Mark*.
4 False. Mark and Stella are at the *meeting point*.
5 False. Harry is in the *car park*. (*Andreas* is at the information desk.)

Use **photocopiable 1** to practise airport vocabulary.

- Have students get into pairs. Tell them that they are detectives and they have to work with their partners to find three people and one dog at an airport.
- Hand out the sheets (one per pair) face down. Once all the pairs have a copy, they can turn it over and start looking. Who can find Bob, Mark, Max and Fifi first? (Answers: Bob=28, Mark=15, May=2, Fifi=20)
- You could also use this sheet to practise numbers with your students: *Where is ... number 4? (At the information point!)*

6 A matching exercise for some more vocabulary. Get your students to work together on this one. There are a number of possible answers but see suggestions below.

1 American	football	5 Italian	pasta
2 French	bistros	6 Japanese	sushi
3 German	sausage	7 Russian	vodka
4 Irish	coffee	8 Swiss	chocolate

7 Five short dialogues with some common nationalities. There are some nice visual clues to help your students. Point out that – unlike in German – nationalities are written with a capital letter in English.

1 Italian 2 Swiss 3 French 4 Russian 5 Canadian

8 **And finally ...** The students look at some well-known international companies and organizations. Let them work together on this one. The students may be surprised by the pronunciation of VW in English – not quite as snappy as it is in German!

1 KLM (the Dutch airline)
2 VW (the German car manufacturer)
3 BBC (British Broadcasting Corporation), CNN (Cable News Network)
4 CIA (Central Intelligence Agency), FBI (Federal Bureau of Investigation)

Extension activity: For more practice on saying the letters, have your students think of some more well-known organizations. They write them down and then take turns reading them out while the others in the class say what they stand for, e.g. *K-G-B! (Ah, It's a Russian organization!) A-R-D. (It's a German television company!)* If they are having problems thinking of similar abbreviations, you may like to offer: UK, USA, VIP, DJ ...

C Please go to gate 4!

coursebook pages 14–15

1 Students can work in pairs or small groups to match up the cities and the countries. Some of them may not be aware that some German cities have different names in English.

Key:

Austria	Vienna
The Czech Republic	Prague
Germany	Cologne & Munich
Great Britain	London
Greece	Athens
Italy	Milan, Rome & Venice
Russia	Moscow
Switzerland	Geneva

2 Some of your students may know the numbers in English, others may not. If you feel your students need some practice before they do this activity, you could spend some time helping them. When they are ready they can use the data on the departure board to match the flights and gates.

Key:

Athens	twelve	Prague	twenty
London	seventeen	Venice	four
Moscow	three	Vienna	six
Munich	eight		

In the second part of the exercise the students match the flights and departure times. At airports, most people would use digital time, i. e. 9:30 = *nine thirty* rather than *half past nine*. 10:00 would be pronounced *ten o'clock*.

Key:

Cologne	B	Athens	C
Geneva	A	Rome	D
Milan	E	Prague	F

3 **1.6** Listening comprehension. The students look at the information board and listen to see if the information in the announcements (not on the board) is correct or incorrect.

Key:

1 False. (*Gate 17*, not gate 14)
2 False. (*SU 964*, not SU 946)
3 True.
4 False. (*QF 243*, not SR 722)

4 1.7 In this listening task, the students add missing information to an information board.

A Gate: 21
B Time: 11:05
C Time: 11:35 Gate: 13

5 A quick game that your students can play in pairs. They can use the sentences in the sample dialogue and any other vocabulary they have picked up. Model the exercise with one student before they go into pairs. Don't forget to listen in on as many conversations as possible.

6 A geography quiz for your students. Let them work together on this.

1 Milan, Venice
2 Detroit, Orlando, Seattle
3 Hong Kong, Kyoto, Mumbai, Shanghai

Use **photocopiable 2** to practise country and city names.

- Make copies and cut each one into four parts.
- Have students work in groups of 2–3. Hand out Cards A and D to half of the groups and Cards B and C to the other half.
- The students in each group then work together to think of the countries and capitals that are missing on their cards.
- In the second phase of the activity, match each group up with a group that has the opposite cards. Without showing each other their cards, students check each other's answers: *We think the capital of Russia is ... Moscow. (That's right.)*

7 Reading comprehension with some short texts about Germany, Britain and Switzerland. While your students may ask you for some of the vocabulary, they are unlikely to need it to do the task. You could encourage them not to worry too much about the words they don't know – and to concentrate on the ones they do!

1 Britain
2 Switzerland
3 Germany, Britain
4 Germany
5 museums

8 **And finally ...** A task in which students test each other's knowledge of vocabulary. Following the model in the book, they ask each questions about words they have seen in the unit, which is a nice way of recycling the vocabulary. You can ask your students: *What's 'I don't know' in German?* They will almost certainly get the answer right!

2

At the end of unit 2 your students should:

- be able to tell the time and talk about their schedule for the week.
- be able to make positive statements in the simple present.
- be able to use *there is* and *there are* correctly.
- be able to talk about festivals, towns and what's on TV.
- be able to talk about things they like and don't like.
- have practised indefinite articles (*a, an*) and regular plurals.
- be able to talk about the things they *always*, *normally*, *sometimes*, *never* do.

A What's the time?

coursebook pages 18–19

1 A nice introduction to times, numbers and countries. If you have some 'geography experts', the other students may like to test their knowledge: *What country is west of Egypt? What country is east of Spain?* etc.

F India	C Japan	D Brazil
G New Zealand	A Scotland	
B Portugal	E South Africa	

2 Students look again at the countries in exercise 1 and see which group can put them in the designated order most quickly.

Group A	Scotland, South Africa, India, Japan, New Zealand, Brazil, Portugal
Group B	New Zealand, Japan, India, South Africa, Scotland, Portugal, Brazil

3 You might want your students to work in pairs on this one. Before they start, make sure that they understand how the colourcoding on the time zone map works.

1 Greece   2 Poland

4 This should cause quite a bit of debate among your students. Even in German some people would struggle with this, but as long as they are practising their times, don't worry too much.

1 six o'clock in the morning	4 12 o'clock (or midday)
2 ten o'clock in the morning	5 ten o'clock in the evening
3 12 o'clock at night (or midnight)	6 any town in Alaska (e.g. Anchorage)

5 Draw a clock on the board and use arrows to explain *past* and *to* before having students do this exercise. Note that some students might say *half past six* for the third one due to interference from German.

5.05 It's five past five.
5.25 It's twenty-five past five.
5.30 It's half past five.
5.45 It's quarter to six.
5.50 It's ten to six.

Make sure students use *in the morning* or *in the afternoon* (or am or pm) and not the 24-hour clock to say what time it is.

Use **photocopiable 3** to give your students more practice in saying clock times.

- Make copies of the three cards – A, B and C – and hand out one per student.
- Before students look at their cards, pre-teach: *clean my teeth, leave the house* and *get up*.
- Students then look at their cards and write down the times that they do the various activities (left column).
- Then they mill around and find someone who has a card with a different letter. They read a sentence such as *I get up at half past six. And you?* (This avoids the more complex *What time do you get up?*) The second student replies *Me too!* or, more probably *Oh, I get up at seven o'clock* and this information is written on the card (right column). Make sure your students speak to each other rather than look at each other's cards.

6 A straightforward matching exercise.

Extension activity: For your stronger students, can they think of other collocation phrases? For example, what else can they watch (a film, birds) or what can they play (basketball, badminton)?

1 C watch TV
2 D play football
3 E go to the cinema
4 B relax at home
5 A have an English class

This will encourage your students to use the structures they have just formed. No answer key here as each student will have a different answer.

7 1.10 A nice listening exercise for your students. Note that the events that Brian and Andy discuss are events that happen on a regular basis, which is why they use the simple present.

Brian:	Wednesday	(go to the) cinema with Jane and Paul at 6.20 pm
Andy:	Wednesday Friday	(play) football from 7–9 pm

8 Students unjumble the sentences, then work in pairs to ask each other the questions.

Key	1 – Is today Friday?	– No, today is Thursday.
	2 – Is your English class on Monday?	– No, my English class is on Wednesday.
	3 – What is your favourite day?	– My favourite day is Monday.

If your students are having trouble with the days of the week, draw a time line on the board and get them to help you put the days in the right order.

9 **And finally ...** a quick bit of revision of both times and geography. Your stronger/faster students can make up some more questions along the same lines.

Key: 5 Tokyo

B How about that?

coursebook pages 20–21

1 A simple exercise to familiarize students with various forms of entertainment. Pre-teach: *terrible*, *colleagues*.

Not everybody will agree on what entertainment is appropriate for the three groups.

Key: Suggested answers:

1 a family with children: magic show, cinema

2 a group of teenagers: rock concert, comedy show, cinema

3 a group of business colleagues after work: all of them

2 Students identify five posters from the Edinburgh festivals. If you can, have students who have been to or who have heard of the festivals work with students who haven't.

a theatre and comedy festival	3	a book festival	2
a music, opera and theater festival	4	a multicultural festival	5
a film festival	1		

3 **1.11** Jack and Sue discuss their work and a few personal details. The task itself is not difficult, particularly if you read the questions through with your students first and check that they understand the meaning of *where* and *who*. (The language box highlights this common mistake for German speakers – confusing *where* (≠ wer) and *who* (≠ wo).) You may like to pre-teach the words: *(business) card, organizer*. Remind students that they don't have to understand every word.

Key: 1 Jack 2 Sue 3 Scotland

4 1.12 We continue to listen to Jack and Sue. They use many of the words the students practised in exercise 3. You may like to pre-teach: *really, famous, before*.

Festivals mentioned: 1, 6, 7, 8, 9 and 10.

5 1.11 Playing the same conversation from exercise 3 will build up your students' confidence as this time they will understand even more.

Scottish Tourism, South Africa, Edinburgh, festival organizer

6 Before students do this grammar exercise, have them study the sample sentences in the grammar box. Draw their attention to the third person *s*.

1 works	3 like	5 love	7 is
2 thinks	4 are	6 comes	8 likes

7 A nice exercise where the students simply have to work out logical sentences – though they will (hopefully) smile at some of the illogical ones. No answer key as there are many different possibilities.

Photocopiable 4 gives your students the chance to practise *Is there?* and *Are there?* as question forms.

- Distribute tables, making sure the 'Student C' one goes to your stronger students.
- Students can do this exercise as pairwork, or they can move around the class, asking as many different people their questions as possible.
- You may like to get them to ask you a couple of questions first to make sure they know how to do it – and also so that they get an idea of how to respond naturally: *Yes, there is/are. No, there isn't/aren't.*

8 There are enough cognates in this reading exercise to make this seemingly difficult text quite easy. Students from countries other than Germany may need a little extra help here. In any case, pre-teach *How many?*

1 There are five or six good Japanese restaurants.

2 There are hundreds of Chinese restaurants.

Extension exercise: Ask your students questions and get them to discuss the restaurants available in their area: *Is there a good Greek restaurant near here? Are there many good Chinese restaurants in [your town]?* Avoid using *any* in your questions as this won't be dealt with until later in the book.

9 **And finally ...** Students get a chance to talk about themselves while practising some of the key structures in Part B.

> **Alternative:** Get the students to share the information in groups. Then ask one person in each group to tell the class about the most interesting things they heard.

C What's on TV tonight?

coursebook pages 22–23

1 Before students do this matching exercise, make sure they can pronounce the TV programmes. Encourage the students to work together – at least to check their answers.

Key: 1 F 2 J 3 C 4 D 5 I 6 E 7 H 8 L 9 K 10 B 11 G 12 A

> **Extension exercise:** Ask your students for examples of each kind of programme.

In the second part of the warmer, students discuss their own likes and dislikes.

> **Alternative:** Students complete the sentences and tell their partner which sentences are true for them. The partner then tells a small group, and the teacher gets feedback from the groups, rather than from everyone.
> In the feedback session, make sure the third person *s* is used: *Peter likes ...*
> Remind students that they can use these phrases *(I like ... I hate ... I have a favourite ...)* to talk about anything: film stars, food, music, etc.

2 **How often?** A nice personalization exercise which encourages students to use adverbs of frequency to talk about themselves. Make sure they have looked at the grammar box before starting.

3 **1.13** Connie and Paul discuss their weekend activities. You may like to pre-teach *I'm sure/ I'm not sure* and *favourite* and have students read the list of activities *before* listening.

Key:

Weekend activities	Connie	Paul
watch TV	✓	✓
relax at home		✓
go swimming	✓	
go shopping		✓
go to the cinema	✓	✓
go to the pub	✓	
go to a concert	✓	

4 This little exercise will help your students practise the correct word order. Before they start, have them look at the grammar box again and try to work out the word order for themselves. Look out for students saying *Connie goes normally* as that's not the correct word order in English.

1 Connie normally goes to the cinema on Sunday evening.
2 Paul normally goes shopping on Saturday.
3 Connie goes jogging on Sunday morning then has lunch with a friend.
4 Paul sometimes stays at home and watches TV.

5 Before students do this matching exercise practising *a* and *an*, have them read the sample sentences in the grammar box. Can they tell you why some words take *a* and some take *an*? Some might notice that words that begin with a vowel take *an* and those that begin with a consonant take *a*. This is almost the whole answer, only it is the vowel sound which is important. So for a word like university, it is *a university* as the sound is a *y* not a *u*.

Now turn to the exercise, pre-teach *series* and be prepared to help the students if they don't have the 'cultural' knowledge.

1 C 2 A 3 D 4 B

6 Nice, near-authentic material at a very low level. Pre-teach *What's on (TV tonight)?*

1 It's on at 6.30 pm (on BBC2).
2 It's 'In the Zoo' at 11.30 pm.
3 It's on ITV (at 7 o'clock).
4 It's on at 11 pm (on ITV).
5 It's 'Eastenders'.

Extension exercise: Students ask each other questions about the schedule. For example: *I like game shows. Is there a game show on tonight? Is there a good programme on at 9 o'clock?*

7 **And finally ...** A nice personalization exercise to end the unit. No answer key as the students come up with their own answers.

3

At the end of unit 3 your students should:

- be able to talk about holidays and leisure activities.
- be able to use the *I like* + *-ing* structure.
- have practised regular and irregular plurals.
- have looked at months of the year.
- have learnt vocabulary connected with clothing and holiday preparation.
- be able to use *this/that* and *these/those* correctly.
- have practised the *th* sound.

A See the world!

coursebook pages 26–27

1 Students discuss their holiday activities. You may like to pre-teach *relax* and *climbing* (make sure they don't pronounce the b). With the students working in pairs or groups, you can listen in on their conversations.

2 Read through the useful language box before having students do this exercise. You might need to help them with some vocabulary: *buy, lie, diving, tent*. Note some students will want to say *make photos*, which does not collocate in English. And a *sea* is not a *lake*.

Key:

buy – souvenirs	lie – on a beach	visit – friends
go – camping	swim – in the sea/ocean	
go – diving	take – photos	

Key:

1 I have three cameras. I **take** lots of p**hotos**.

2 Tents are great! We **go camping** with friends in the summer.

3–5 Open answers

3 A matching exercise giving the students the chance to discuss different types of holidays. Be prepared to explain *expensive* and *forest* and to help with pronunciation.

Key:

1C	City breaks	5A	Active holidays
2G	Cultural holidays	6E	Beach holidays
3B	Exotic holidays	7F	Camping holidays
4D	Luxury holidays		

4 This exercise gives students the opportunity to express their own opinions about holidays.

When they ask their partner, encourage them to use the *And you?* structure. For example: *I don't like lying in the sun. I think it's boring. And you?* The students should take it in turns to read out the sentences.

5 Quick practice of the *-ing* form and base form. Have students look at the structure in the grammar box first. Then encourage them to help each other fill the gaps.

1 relaxing	4 go	7 read
2 watch	5 relax	8 going
3 reading	6 watching	

6 **1.15** The students will hear a dialogue between Alan and Carole about holidays. Encourage them to use the *like* + *-ing* structure in their answers.

Alan likes ...	Carol likes ...
sleeping in a tent/camping	lying on the beach
visiting museums and local culture	staying in expensive (5 star) hotels

Use **photocopiable 5** to practise holiday vocabulary.

- Make enough copies so that each pair has one copy.
- Get the students to look at the illustrations. Help them if they don't know some of the words in English.
- Explain we are going to help Martin and Valentino choose where to go on holiday.
- It is a good idea to talk them through the first example. The point system is like the voting system in the Eurovision Song contest, with 5 for the best, then 4, 3, 2 and 1.
- In pairs, the students work through the examples, adding points in the table.
- There may be some examples where some countries don't get any points. (For example, it is not possible to swim in the sea in the Czech Republic.)
- The students then count up the points for each country. Have they all chosen the same country or are there differences? They can compare notes with other pairs.

7 A nice sequencing activity, which will be different for different students. You may like to pre-teach *to decide, to pack, keys*. Your students may also need the words *First of all, then, next*, and *finally* when discussing their lists. Encourage the students to compare sequences as there are likely to be some differences.

8 **And finally ...** Students end the section by telling each other about the souvenirs they have collected (and perhaps showing them if they have brought something to class). This is a good chance to review country names and also gives the class an opportunity to chat freely at the end of the lesson.

B Unusual holidays

coursebook pages 28–29

1 Your students may not know all of the answers to the quiz so be prepared to give them some help. For example, 2: *The country was called Rhodesia, but today it is ...*

1 A 2 E 3 B 4 C 5 D

2 A short reading about sharks. The students have to choose between two verbs. You may like to pre-teach *shark, coast, experience* and *necessary*.

1 see	4 live	7 relax	10 take
2 go	5 know	8 are	
3 come	6 have	9 give	

3 An exercise to raise awareness of plurals in English. A common mistake for German speakers is to say: *There were ten* persons *at my party last night*. The word *person* is only used in formal situations, often on notices – for example in a lift: *Max. ten persons*.

Sharks, animals, penguins, seals, boats, photos

4 A simple exercise to give the students confidence using singular or plural forms – and pick up some more interesting facts about sharks!

1 sharks	3 metres	5 types
2 Sharks, people	4 attacks	6 shark

5 **1.16** A listening exercise to familiarize students with the months in English. The first time they listen, the students only have to listen out for the months.

Students will hear every month except February.

During the second listening (and third, if needed), students complete the gaps.

South Africa:	October, September
Kenya:	July
Zimbabwe:	March, April

Extension activity: All change! Get your students to arrange themselves according to their birthdays (not date of birth!) So the person whose birthday is closest to January the 1st sits (or stands) on the left, and the person whose birthday is closest to December the 31st sits (or stands) on the right. It is quite common for two students to discover that they have the same birthday. This is also a nice way to get them to work with a new partner.

6 A simple reading text. Your students shouldn't worry about one or two unknown words as long as they can answer the questions.

1 It's in East Africa.

2 It's famous for Mount Kilimanjaro, the Serengeti National Park and the Masai Mara National Reserve.

3 The big problem is water.

7 **Sounds good.** This is an awareness exercise. Students will notice the Ws and Vs in various words. If they are having problems, you can read out the first sentence, stressing the W and V sounds. Note that in sentence 3 there is a W sound in *ever**y**one*.

1 C 2 D 3 B 4 A

8 **And finally ...** No answer key here. Hopefully your students will come up with some interesting ideas. If they need some help, perhaps you can mention your idea of a great holiday first.

C Out of this world

coursebook pages 30–31

1 A simple matching exercise to familiarize your students with some more vocabulary.

Items on the conveyor belt starting on the right and going clockwise:
dictionary, tickets, sunglasses, dress, T-shirt, credit card, swimming costume, mp3 player, passport, umbrella, shirt, mobile phone, jeans, laptop, shoes, shorts

documents	tickets, passport
clothes	dress, T-shirt, swimming costume, shirt, jeans, shoes, shorts
technology	mp3 player, mobile phone, laptop
other	dictionary, sunglasses, credit card, umbrella

2 A fun game to play with your students to practice *this, that, these* and *those*. Perhaps best not to let them put expensive jewellery or wallets on the desk! In fact, you might want to bring your own items to class such as sweets, markers or coins. Explain how we use the plural for *glasses*.

3 **1.17** **Sounds good.** An exercise to raise awareness of the subtle difference between the *th* sound in clo**th**es and **th**anks. Personally, I don't lose too much sleep when my students can't hear the difference.

Clothes [ð]	**Thanks** [θ]
this	thing
that	theatre
these	thousand
those	

Photocopiable 6 allows your students to practise *this, that, these*, and *those* while reviewing nationalities and other simple adjectives.

- Make enough photocopies so there is one copy between two students.
- Explain to that they have to find as many sentence pairs as they can. Each sentence should use *this/that* or *these/those* and compare people or objects that are on this side of the canal with ones on the other side.
- Give them a time limit. If you have a competitive class, you could turn this into a competition. Which pair of students is fastest or finds the most (valid) sentence pairs within a specific time limit?

4 A bit of grammar for your students. They have to decide which verb form is correct in the sentences about tourism. You might want to quickly revise the rules for verb + *s*.

1 creates
2 is
3 becomes
4 are
5 make
6 are

In the second part of the exercise, the students should say whether they think the facts about tourism are positive or negative. They can discuss this in a simple way with their partner.

5 The language in this short text is pretty simple with many words that the students know already.

1 He is an American multimillionaire and the first space tourist.
2 He is the first man to pay to go into space.
3 No, there are no hotels in space.
4 It is very, very expensive.

6 Following on from the text in exercise 5, the students have enough language to understand the statements and indicate their opinion by making four crosses on the chart. We don't expect them to produce this language at this stage, but they should be able to deal with it receptively. There are no answers here as the students express their own opinions.

7 **1.18** Listening comprehension. Carla and Paul talk about their holiday plans.

Paul	This year: Spain The year before: Spain	
Carla	This year: Greece? Egypt? Last year: France The year before that: Tanzania	

Paul has a problem with what to take.

Carla has a problem with where to go and where to stay.

8 A quick exercise for students to express their own views on what is easy and difficult about travel arrangements. They should be able to discuss this in a simple way with their partners. They have some useful phrases given at the underneath the second part of the exercise.

9 **And finally ...** Students exchange information about their last holiday. Although this involves the past tense, it is unlikely that it will trouble many students. They can use some of the language in the box below.

4

At the end of unit 4 your students should:

- be able to talk about their daily routines.
- have practised adverbs of time.
- be familiar with the simple present tense and be able to form questions with *do/does*.
- be able to use short answers in response to simple present questions.
- be familiar with the past tense of the verb *to be* in questions and answers.
- be able to talk about their last holiday.
- have practised phrases with the words *both* and *neither*.

A A great lifestyle

coursebook pages 34–35

1 A simple exercise to start things off – putting daily activities into a logical sequence. Different students will have different views, which, of course, is fine.

Key: Sample sequence:

1 get up
2 have a shower
3 have breakfast
4 go to work
5 turn on the computer
6 send emails
7 have lunch
8 have dinner
9 watch TV
10 go to bed

While the students are doing the second part of the exercise, make sure you move around and listen in on their conversations.

2 **1.20** Listening comprehension. Your students listen to Betty and Carl talking about their routines. They need to listen carefully and add the information to the table. They then add their own information to the table. After exercise 3 you can have them work in pairs to ask each other about their routines.

Key:

	Betty		Carl	
Wake up	yes	6.30	no	around 7.00
Leave home	yes	shortly before 7.35	no	he works at home
Check email	yes	3 times a day	no	no mention of email
Finish work	no	between 5.30 and 6.30	no	he's always at work

3 **1.20** Your students listen to Betty and Carl talking about their routines for a second time. This time they need to listen carefully and add the missing words to the dialogue.

Key:

1 do you, I do
2 do you, Do you, I don't
3 do you
4 Do you
5 Do you have, No, I don't

Extension activity: The blue box gives your students the short answer form for 'do' questions. Get your students to ask each other lots of 'do' questions. Whoever answers five questions correctly gets a round of applause. Perhaps at the end they can ask *you* lots of 'do' questions. Remember, you don't have to tell the truth.

4 **Key verb: leave.** Students make sentences all based on the verb to leave. Allow them to work together on this one. You may like to pre-teach *alone, busy* and *waste*.

What time do you/leave home/in the morning?
Please/leave me alone./I am busy.
My train/leaves at 3 pm/this afternoon.
I am always/the last person to leave/the office.
Don't/leave the TV on/all night. It's a waste.
Some people/leave everything/to the last minute. I think that's bad planning.

'Find someone who' is a fun activity. Get students to move around the room and ask as many people as possible. Feel free to join in both asking and answering questions. Before you start, you may want to make sure they can convert the statements into questions.

5 This little exercise allows your students to familiarize themselves with correct word order in simple present questions. Encourage them to work together.

1 Do you always have breakfast?
2 Do you normally have a shower in the morning?
3 Do you drink coffee after 10.30 p.m.?
4 Do you live near your family or friends? (or 'friends or family')
5 Do you watch TV in the evening?
6 Do you go on holiday in the summer?

Use **photocopiable 7** to give the students more practice with the simple present.

- There are ten 'Find someone who' cards on the photocopiable so make enough copies so that each student has one card.
- Before students begin, explain that they should formulate questions and read them to their classmates, not show them their card. You may like to model one question if you think they may have problems. Note that they have the opportunity to complete one question in any way they want; they should do this before the activity starts.
- During the exercise, students mingle and ask each other questions. Whenever they get a positive response, they should write that person's name on the right line.
- In the feedback session, ask your students about anything interesting they found out. You may need to remind them of the 3rd person *s*.

6 A nice activity introducing the phrase *sort of* together with simple questions. Your students may ask if they should use the plural or singular form in the question. For uncountable nouns (food) it is clearly singular. For countable nouns it depends on whether you expect the answer to be singular or plural. For example: *What sort of car do you drive?* (You expect the person only has one car.) *What sort of films do you like?* (You expect the person likes more than one kind of film.)

1 What sort of films do you like?
2 What sort of TV programmes do you like?
3 What sort of car do you drive?
4 What sort of holidays do you like?
5 What sort of things do you do at the weekend? (Note that Americans say *on the weekend.*)
6–8 open answers

Mingle with your students as they ask and answer the questions. Join in the exercise with them and keep the language as natural as possible. They should be interested in the replies, not just doing an exercise.

7 **And finally ...** Students write five questions that they hope will elicit the answer *Yes, I do* from their partner.

B Tell me about it!

coursebook pages 36–37

1 Students work in pairs to identify these buildings and sites, and then try to say more about the countries in which they are located. Tell students not to worry if they only know two or three of the places: they should just do the best they can.

1 Taj Mahal
2 Sagrada Familia Cathedral
3 Burj al Arab hotel
4 Machu Picchu
5 Chrysler building

	location	food	language	weather
1	India	curry	many different ones	hot
2	Spain	paella	Catalan	Mediterra- nean climate
3	Dubai	halal meat and rice	Arabic	very hot
4	Peru	potatoes and corn	Spanish	mild
5	USA	burgers and hot dogs	English	hot summers, cold winters

2 A quick **language quiz** for the students to do in pairs.

1 That's possible.
2 I don't know.
3 When we say goodbye.
4 Sometimes.
5 In parts of Africa.
6+7 Many answers possible.

3 1.21 Your students will hear a radio interview with Dave, a public opinion researcher. It is a fairly long interview so you may want to stop the recording a few times.

He talks about: 1, 3, 4, 6, 7, 8

You may need to play the recording again for the second part of the exercise.

Dave likes his work. He likes the fact that it is always different. He likes meeting people
Dave doesn't like it when people don't want to talk to him. He doesn't like working in bad weather.

4 1.21 This little exercise concentrates on the question forms that Dave used in his interview. Your students might not need to hear the recording again, but they might find it useful for checking their answers.

1 do you watch on
2 car do you
3 Do you think, have too much

Once they have written the questions, they can answer or ask their partners the questions.

Use **photocopiable 8** to practise questions with *does*.

- Make one copy for every three students and cut the sheets into the three parts.
- Arrange your students in groups of three (Students A, B and C) and hand the first part to the 'A' students in each group.
- The 'A' students should ask as many questions as they can while the 'B' and 'C' students try to answer. Make sure the latter listen to the questions, not read them.
- After a couple minutes, hand out a second part to the 'B' students and have the groups repeat the process. Then do the same with the third part.
- Make sure you listen in on the questions and answers. Make a note of some of your favourites.

5 Some simple questions for your students. Encourage them to give a short answer plus a little information as just the bare short answer can sound robotic.

6 Reading comprehension – a hotel review. The students simply have to match the comments with the categories, then answer some questions.

Key:

1 food
2 room
3 cost
4 location
5 check-in

Key:

1 No, it wasn't. It was 3 km from the centre.
2 No, it wasn't. It was really cheap.
3 It was cold.
4 No, it wasn't. The staff were English.

Although the students have seen it before (in Unit 3, Part C), the grammar box has a quick summary of the simple past form of *to be*.

7 A simple matching exercise, giving students more practice of *was* and *were*.

Key: 1 C 2 B 3 A 4 D 5 E

8 Still with the theme of hotels. The students have to decide whether the statements are positive, negative, or possibly both. No answer key as the answers will vary by student.

9 **And finally ...** A fun exercise in which the students have the answers and have to supply the questions. Before students get in pairs, you might want to have them look again at the grammar boxes in Part B on how to form questions.

C What makes you happy?

coursebook pages 38–39

1 In this exercise your students look at the phrases and see if they can find a photo which matches one of the thoughts. They may also like to look at the photos and discuss what the woman is thinking. The point is not to try and match up all the photos with the thoughts; it's to discuss feelings and emotions.

Key:

Some suggestions to get you started:
Thought 1 could go with photo E or M.
Thought 2 could go with photo K.
Thought 3 could go with photo F.
Thought 4 could go with photo M or N.
Thought 5 could go with photo B.

Students then find opposites.

new – old	terrible – great
stressed – calm and relaxed	sad – happy
intelligent – stupid	boring – interesting

2 Completing the dialogues. Your students use the opposites from exercise 1. More than one answer is possible – here are some suggestions:

1 boring
2 terrible/great
3 Calm and relaxed, calm and relaxed
4 boring/interesting
For me, history and English were boring/interesting.

After the gapfill exercise, the students can ask each other the questions.

3 The students make sentences about the sounds, smells and tastes they love – and hate.

4 Now the students get to work with partners and find out about, then report on, things they like and hate. Before they start, model the question to point out the difference between *Do you ...?* and *Does your partner ...?*

5 You might want your students to work with a different partner to do this exercise.

6 Both or neither? Students can look at the grammar box before matching the questions and answers.

1 F 2 B 3 C 4 A 5 E 6 D (or F)

7 1.22 A listening exercise. Your students will hear people talking about lifestyles.

Paul: enjoys physical activities, goes to the gym, meets friends (maybe!)
Ian: eats hamburgers, likes computer games, meets friends, watches films
Kelly: meets friends, walks a lot, watches films, works hard

In the second part of the exercise, students can make their own sentences using *both of them* and *neither of them*.

Suggested answers:

Kelly & Ian	Both of them watch films.
Paul & Kelly	Neither of them likes computer games.
Ian & Paul	Both of them meet friends. OR: Neither of them works hard.

8 **And finally ...** A nice personalization exercise at the end of the lesson. Give the students a minute or two to think about the topics and then get them to talk in small groups.

Journal I

See notes in the teaching tips (page 10) on ways to use the material in the journals.

Coursebook pages 42–49

Are you talking to me?

Before reading

- Your students get into groups and think of as many different languages as they can. Which group has the longest list? Then they can look at the list of languages Lisa encountered on her travels and see how many were on their list.

After reading

- **Where's that?** The students discuss where they think the four pictures may have been taken. The correct answer is not important; it is the discussion that counts.
- **Internet research:** Those students who have internet access may like to visit Lisa's website and report back to the others about what they found.

From where I stand

Before reading

- The students look at the photos and discuss where they might have been taken. They can do this in pairs or small groups.

After reading

- **What language?** The students can read where the photos were taken. Let them discuss what languages are spoken in the countries.
- **I want to go to ... :** The students decide where they would like their feet to be – inspired by Lisa's photos.

City Break: Berlin

Before reading

- Get your students to discuss what they know about Berlin and what they would like to know about Berlin. (For those who live in Berlin, they may like to think of unusual things about Berlin that people not from Berlin may find interesting or surprising.) While they are reading they can check to confirm their ideas, or, hopefully, get the answers to some of their questions.

After reading

- **Facts and figures:** Let the students look at the information about Berlin. You then pretend that you don't know anything about the city and ask your students to tell you something about its population, sports, things to see, places to eat.

- **Photos:** The students can discuss what is in the photos. Have they been to those places/ eaten that dish? Is it a good place to go/food to eat?

- **24 hours:** The students have 24 hours in Berlin (or have a visitor for 24 hours). Where would they go? They can discuss an itinerary with their classmates. Which group can think of the best itinerary?

Numbers

Before reading

- **Important numbers:** Write down four numbers on the board. Tell the students that these numbers are important to you. They can then ask simple questions to find out why they are important. For example: *Do you have four children? Is your house number 4?*

After reading

- **Find me a word:** Ask the students to find you a word which begins with one particular letter. The first student to find one can choose the next letter. This is a nice way to interact with the text without having to read it all.

- **In my country:** The students look at some of the facts and discuss what the figure may be for their own country. For example: *Here in Switzerland we laugh 20 times a day!*

Pipe guys take over the world?!

Before reading

- Ask your students to brainstorm where you can see pipes. Which group can write the longest list? You may need to help with the vocabulary.

After reading

- **Favourites:** The students choose their favourite pipe guy and tell their partner why they like that one.

Dinner is ready

Before reading

- Ask your students to look at the photo of the garage and ask: *What can you see in the garage? How does it make you feel?* They can discuss in groups.

After reading

- **Keep or throw away:** The students write down all the things in the story that Penny was not happy about and the things that Gary wanted to keep. They should write them down on separate pieces of paper. Then, as a group, they have to decide whether they would keep or throw away each of the things. It will be interesting to see whether the men's and women's lists are different, and if so, how.

5

At the end of unit 5 your students should:
- be able to use the simple past.
- be familiar with regular forms and common irregular forms of the past tense.
- have talked about many events in the past, both historical and personal.
- be able to use short answers in response to simple past questions.
- have practised using *ago*.

A What a week!

coursebook pages 50–51

1 A simple quiz to start things off and to practise *was*. It will be interesting to see what your students know about the various people.

1 Neil (Armstrong)	American, pilot, walked on moon on 20 July, 1969, became a teacher after his career as an astronaut
2 Alexander (Graham Bell)	Scottish inventor, his mother and wife were deaf, died in 1922
3 Amelia (Earhart)	American, born in 1897, probably died in the Pacific Ocean, wrote a lot of popular books about flying
4 Barack (Obama)	Born in 1961 in Honolulu, studied at Harvard Law School, speaks Indonesian, plays basketball
5 Marie (Curie)	Born in 1867, grew up in Warsaw but moved to Paris, her daughter also won a Nobel prize
6 Joanne (Murray) (JK Rowling)	Born in 1965, grew up in England, worked as an English teacher in Portugal in the early 1990s

2 Students can look at the grammar box on the simple past and read the example sentences. They then match up the present tense and past tense forms of some common irregular verbs. Model and practise the pronunciation of the past tense forms in box B.

buy – bought	play – played
come – came	wait – waited
say – said	live – lived
see – saw	work – worked
think – thought	listen – listened

3 This little exercise allows your students to familiarize themselves with some of the vocabulary in the texts which follow. Point out that the three famous people referred to are the ones in exercise 4 (and don't give them the answers until after they've read the texts). You may like to pre-teach *to become* and its past tense form *became*.

4 It is important for your students to realize that they don't have to understand every word – as long as they have enough to find the information they are looking for. The answers to exercise 3 are as follows:

🔑
1 JK Rowling
2 Barak Obama
3 JK Rowling
4 Amelia Earhart
5 Barak Obama

5 Students then find some more simple past forms in the three texts. Note that the verbs in the list are not in the same order as in the texts.

🔑
become – became (line 5)
go – went (line 4)
teach – taught (line 5)
win – won (line 6)
have – had (line 18)
disappear – disappeared (line 12)
live – lived (line 15)
work – worked (line 15)
start – started (line 9)
want – wanted (line 9)
save – saved (line 9)
try – tried (line 12)

6 A nice personalization activity which will encourage the students to use the past tense in a very simple way.

🔑 Model answers:
1 When I was young I lived with my parents in a house in Leipzig.
2 I went to school in 1974. It was a primary school in Essen.
3 At school I liked biology and sports.
4 I worked for BASF in Ludwigshafen for 12 years.
5 Last week I bought a new bicycle.

7 Matching questions and answers. The students have to add an appropriate verb and match up the questions and answers.

🔑
1 D bought
2 B came
3 C did
4 A thought

8 **1.23** The students will hear Pat talking about things on her 'to do' list. They have to tick the activities she did.

🔑 She had lunch with Sally and she played tennis with Sam.

Use **photocopiable 9** to give your students more exposure to past tense forms.

- Make enough copies so that there is one for each pair of students. Cut each copy in half.
- Put the students in pairs of A and B students and give them their version of the secret diary. The students then have to complete the gaps in the diary by *speaking* to each other (not reading the other person's text).
- The more advanced students may use the correct question forms but it likely that most students will just read the sentence and wait for their partner to fill the gap.

9 More personalization using the past tense form. Once the students have completed the checklist they can tell their partner.

10 Writing practice. The student complete the diary with what they did last weekend, then tell their partner the information. Let them know that it doesn't have to be true! No answer key here as the answer will vary by student.

11 **And finally ...** Students end the section with some more personalization. They can work in pairs and tell their partners about the people they know.

B My life & times

coursebook pages 52–53

1 The important moments in life. Get the students to look at the pictures and think what important event is represented. They should then discuss other important events in people's lives. (See box in exercise 2.)

2 The students can put the events in their life in order, though it may be more interesting for them to work together on this one. The students can ask each other *when did you ...?* and arrange the order for their partners. Note that some people might be sensitive about their age so they can use *I don't want to tell you when I did that, it was so long ago* for times they would rather not talk about more precisely.
Refer them to the grammar box and the example sentences below the box. Point out the use of *ago* + word order (since German speakers tend to say *I went to Australia for 5 years.* – rather than *5 years ago*). There are other useful time words and phrases – in blue print – across the middle of the page.

3 A simple gapfill exercise that shouldn't be too difficult for your students. No answer key here as answers will vary by student. (Although note that the Berlin Wall came down in 1989 (sentence 3).)

4 Get your students to ask their partners these simple past questions. After three questions they can change roles. You can encourage your stronger students to ask further questions based on their partner's responses. *Where did you go on holiday? What did you have for breakfast?* etc.

Extension activity: Get your students to write questions to ask you about your past. Be prepared that some people might ask some personal questions but of course you don't have to tell the truth!

5 A simple gapfill exercise in which the students add a suitable word or phrase. Afterwards they can work in pairs and ask each other the questions.

Suggested answers:

1 go
2 party
3 at the weekend
4 good

6 A reading exercise with some easy past tense forms. You make like to pre-teach *to go bananas*.

buy – bought
find – found
get – got
go – went
say – said
take – took
talk – talked
tell – told
think – thought

Use **photocopiable 10** to help your students retell the story of William and the bank.

- Make a copy and cut out the 12 cards. (If you have a large class, you may have to have the students work in two groups. In that case, you will need two sets of cards.)
- Explain to the students that you want them to retell the story using the 12 pictures.
- Students each get a picture and stand up. They should then discuss their pictures with each other and arrange themselves in the correct order. Once everybody is in the right place, they use their pictures to tell you the story – and hopefully they've got it right!
- If you have a smaller group, they can rearrange the pictures on a table, but encourage them to speak about the story, not just move the pictures in silence.

7 Talking about when things happen. Look at the grammar box with your students and have them read the examples before doing the gapfill.

Model answers:

1 in Hausach
2 at half past nine
3 on Thursday
4 at half past seven

8 **1.24** The students listen to people talking about special moments in their lives. They have to put them in the order they hear them.

Key:
1 getting married
2 winning money
3 a sporting moment
4 success in exams
5 starting a family

9 **And finally ...** The students have the answers and have to write the corresponding questions. Allow them to work together on this one.

Key: Suggested questions:
What did you do on the way to work?/What did you buy this morning?
Did you play basketball?/Did you go swimming?
Did you win?/Did you enjoy it?
Did you call your sister?/Did you do your homework?

Once they have finished, they should mill around and ask their classmates the questions.

C Moments to remember

coursebook pages 54–55

1 **Quick quiz.** Students match the events with the pictures.

Key:
A Germany won the world cup in football.
B The Berlin Wall came down.
C People enjoyed the first colour TV programme.
D The Olympics were in China.
E The Titanic sank.
F The first James Bond film came out ('Dr. No').
G The Vietnam War ended.

2 A fun way for your students to practise their past tense forms. They could also work in small groups for this exercise.

In the second part of the exercises, students work in pairs to ask questions and practise short answers. Have them read through the examples first.

3 **Key verb: remember.** Your students match up sentences with a suitable response, then answer the three questions.

Key: 1 E 2 A 3 B 4 C 5 D 6 F

Personalizing sentences (sample answers):

6 Do you remember where I put my keys/wallet/coursebook?

3 I remember my last birthday party/when the Berlin wall came down.

4 As a warmer for the reading exercise, the students should put the objects in order of value. You might need to help them with some of the words first. The students may have other ideas, but here is a suggestion:

paperclip – pen – doorknob – camping stove – snow globe – meeting with a rockstar – speaking role in a film – skidoo – van – house

In the reading, there will be words that your students probably don't know, but they should be able to work out the order in which Kyle traded the objects.

paperclip – pen – doorknob – camping stove – a skidoo – a white van – an afternoon with Alice Cooper – a snow globe – a speaking role in a film – a house

5 A quick quiz based on the reading text.

1 two ladies
2 in winter
3 movie producer
4 They wanted more people to live in Kipling.

6 A vocabulary-building exercise using words the students have just read in the text. Get your students to work together on this.

1 doorknob
2 to swap
3 stove
4 hits
5 empty
6 role

7 **And finally ...** A short writing exercise in which the students complete four sentences. They should tell the truth for two sentences and invent something for two.

Once they have completed the exercise they can read it to their partners and see whether they can distinguish fact from fiction!

Extension activity: The students write down a number of items in their house that they might want to exchange for something else. Then they talk to other students to find out what they have and discuss whether they want to exchange or not. This is a lighthearted exercise and the students don't have to tell the truth.

6

At the end of unit 6 your students should:

- be able to talk about money.
- have practised the verb *to need.*
- have improved their debating skills.
- know how to use the gerund, e. g. *smoking is bad for you.*
- have practised adjectives, comparatives and superlatives.
- be more aware of how to use stress for emphasis and contrast.
- have practised the 'noun + infinitive' structure.

A Money matters

coursebook pages 58–59

1 A **quick quiz** about money. There are enough visual clues in the photos for your students to work out which currency comes from which country.

1 Zimbabwe	4 India	7 Great Britain
2 Australia	5 China	8 Thailand
3 Mexico	6 USA	

2 Some interesting facts about different currencies. Refer your students to the list of countries in exercise 1 and tell them not to worry if they don't know some of the answers.

Zimbabwe (trillion)	Great Britain (Hong Kong)
Australia (plastic)	India (17 languages)
USA (dead presidents)	China (paper money)
South Africa (Big Five)	

3 Your students look at some phrases about money. Do they agree or disagree with them?

4 The students can read the opinions about money from five different people and they can express their own opinions. Do they agree or disagree? You may like to pre-teach *easier, crazy* and *to save*. There is no answer key but hopefully your students will have opinions on money that they want to express. You can encourage them to use the five phrases in the box below the five people.

5 *Need* is a very useful verb that students can use in a variety of ways. This **key verb** exercise gives them some practice. Two questions after the exercise allow the students to give some personal information (and hopefully use *need*).

1 sleep	3 something	5 help
2 money	4 holiday	6 air

6 This is a nice exercise for students to discuss what is important to them. Get them to work in pairs (or even small groups) to generate a discussion, and encourage them to use the phrases in the box. No answer key as they are expressing their own opinions.

7 The students can do another gapfill, this time using the words *need* and *live/do without*.

1 sun	3 money	5 time
2 food	4 qualifications	6 pen

Use **photocopiable 11** to practise *to need*.

- You can either leave the photocopiable as it is and make one copy for each pair of students, or you can cut the cartoons out. (Make enough for the students to have one each.)
- If you want a gentle exercise, the students look at the activity in pairs and discuss what the various people need. Encourage them to find more than one answer. (During the feedback session, you can see which pair has found the most answers.).
- For a more active exercise, hand out one cartoon to each student. Students then move around the room showing their cartoon to the other students, who have to say what the person in the cartoon needs.

8 **1.26** Listening comprehension. Your students will hear Ed and Rachel talking about money and happiness. Have students look at the table first to help them focus their listening and pre-teach *research* and *rich*. You may need to play the recording more than once.

Ed talks about a holiday and $100,000.

Rachel talks about an article in a newspaper, research in America, rich people and birthday presents.

Both talk about $20,000.

For the second part, the questions are just true/false.

1 F 2 T 3 F 4 T

With the final question, the students can express their own views on whether buying things or buying experiences is more rewarding.

9 **And finally ...** The students can tell their partner about three things: an unwanted present, something that makes them happy and an experience they would like to have. Give them time to think about things before they start speaking. Make sure you listen in on their conversations while they are talking.

Extension activity: Can you be poor and happy? Get the students to brainstorm in groups, what activities you can do with no money at all.

B The things I love

coursebook pages 60–61

1 A quick brainstorming session about things the students love and hate. No answer key as they are expressing their own opinions.

2 The students say what they think about a variety of topics. The topics were chosen as they are things which some people seem to love while others hate them. Clarify any new vocabulary before students work in small groups to put the items into categories.

3 Talking about activities. The gerund is introduced here so you might want to read through the grammar box with your students before they do the two parts of the exercise.

read – reading	have – having	speak – speaking
smoke – smoking	play – playing	fly – flying
go – going	plan – planning	

1 playing	3 Choosing, Flying	5 Speaking
2 reading, going	4 smoking	6 having

4 The students can express their opinions on phrases (which all include the gerund structure). In the second part of the exercise, they are asked to change the sentences (if necessary) so that they are true for them. You may like to help them with the first one, for example: *I think cooking is brilliant! I do it twice a day!*

5 Reading comprehension. The students read the text about Clarke Peters and decide whether he loves or hates the things he talks about. There is quite a bit of new vocabulary in the text but they don't need to understand it all to do the task.

Clarke Peters ...

loves music (even if it makes him cry).
loves good singers.
loves gardening.
loves painting.

hates bad singers.
hates drivers who use their mobiles.
hates being late.

Students unscramble sentences from the text.

1 La Mer is my favourite piece of music.
2 There's nothing better than painting.
3 I hate people who drive in front of you.
4 I hate being late.

6 Get the students to work in small groups for this one. Give them time to think of things that they love or hate and to find a variety of structures that they have looked at in the lesson so far. No answer key as they are expressing their own opinions.

7 You should spend some time practising comparatives and superlatives as they are very important structures. Look at the examples in the grammar box before having students get into pairs to do the exercise – or do the extension exercise below.

1 F 2 A 3 D 4 B 5 C 6 E

Extension activity: Ask your students to stand in order of height. Once they have done this, look at the three tallest students and ask: *Is Michael short? (No, he's tall!) That's right. He is tall. But look at Sabine. She's ... (Taller than Michael!) Very good. But wait a minute. Michael is tall, Sabine is taller, but here's Mustafa. He's the ... (Tallest!).* Make sure you let your students say the target structure (*tall, taller, tallest*) rather than just telling them.
It can be useful for some students if you write the adjective (*tall*) comparative (*taller*) and superlative (*tallest*) on the board as you elicit them.
You can of course also bring objects to class to illustrate the grammar point.

8 Students use superlatives to fill the gaps and then finish the sentences so that they are true for them. There is some flexiblity in how the gaps can be filled. Below are some suggestions.

1 most expensive OR best
2 coldest/hottest
3 best OR coldest/hottest
4 most successful
5 most successful OR best
6 oldest

Use **photocopiable 12** to give your students more practice on comparatives and superlatives.

- For a gentle version, hand out one copy to each pair of students and have them make as many comparative and superlative sentences as possible.
- For a more active version, cut the pictures into strips and hand out the strips, one or two per student. The students then go around the class, showing their strip to other students, who have to form a comparative or superlative sentence.
- For a more active and challenging version, cut out all the pictures. The students should then try to find their two 'partners' without showing their picture to anyone else! Once they have, they should then form the comparative and superlative forms – ideally before they show each other the pictures.

9 **And finally ...** A final exercise allowing your students to be creative with one of the new structures of this section. Here are some suggested answers.

Key:
1 ... learning Latin.
2 ... January.
3 ... cooking fish and chips.
4 ... watching television at home.

C 101 things to do ...

coursebook pages 62–63

1 A quick brainstorming session about things that may be in the book on the page. No answer key here as answers will vary.

2 The students read a short text about the book and fill in an appropriate form of the verb in the gaps. You may like to do the first couple with them to remind them of the gerund and to make sure they are going in the right direction.

Key:
1 visiting
2 writing
3 catching
4 driving
5 getting
6 changing
7 being
8 milking
9 swimming
10 need

3 A simple matching exercise for your students. Nothing too difficult here, though some sentence beginnings have more than one possible ending.

Key: 1 E/A 2 A 3 D/E 4 B 5 C

4 The students can brainstorm what makes their days good and bad.

Key: Model answers:

	Positive things	Negative things
Morning	Eating a good English breakfast	Waking up late for work
Afternoon	Watching a good football game on TV	Working all afternoon
Evening	Having some sweet dreams	Sleeping in a cold bed

5 A good opportunity for students to express their opinions. You may like to model the structure before you get your students to work in pairs or small groups.

6 Reading comprehension. There might be some unknown words for your students, but they shouldn't have too much trouble putting Helen's weekend in the correct order.

1 My perfect weekend in London starts on Friday ...
2 After that we go for dinner to talk about the play or film ...
3 Saturday morning starts with a walk in the park ...
4 In the evening we sometimes go to a classical concert ...
5 I love reading the papers on Sunday morning ...
6 Sunday lunch is often a meal in a pub or a restaurant ...

After the text there are a couple of questions. Encourage your students to discuss the answers with their classmates.

7 1.27 In this **sounds good** exercise, the students have to match up the two parts of the sentence and decide which words are stressed, before listening to the recording to check their answers. Model an example to show which types of words are contrasted and emphasized.

1 C like, hate	3 D lovely, terrible	5 A walk, drove
2 B good, terrible	4 E happy, sad	6 F hot, cold

8 1.28 You might want to start off this listening exercise by asking the students if they would like to take a year off work and, if so, why? The students then listen to a podcast made by a man who decided to take a year off work. The recording is quite long so it is a good idea to stop the recording a few times while you're playing it.

Why a year off?	He wanted a change.
Why a change of plans?	He started a family.

In the second part of the exercise, the students match up the activities and the countries in which he planned to do them.

Visit an ashram	in India
Do a cycling tour	in the south of France
Learn about a greener life	in Scotland
Teach English	in China
Go skydiving	in Spain
Drive down the coast	in the USA

The activity he didn't do was visiting an ashram.

9 **And finally ...** A final exercise allowing your students to be creative. Let's hope they can impress you with their creativity!

7

At the end of unit 7 your students should:

- be able to talk about decisions.
- have discussed things they are either *good at* or *bad at*.
- have practised *someone*, *anyone*, *no one* and *everyone*.
- have practised *how to* and *what to do*.
- have talked about being lucky.
- have looked at negative adjectives.
- have practised reading and saying big numbers.

A That's a difficult decision

coursebook pages 66–67

1 Before students sort the phrases, have them look at the illustration and say what the arrows indicate (clear decision on the left vs. indecision, i.e. I *can't decide/ there are so many option*s on the right). Below are some suggestions to get you started.

Clear decision	Indecision
Right. Good. No problem.	Not sure about that.
That's what I want.	I can't decide ...
Maybe next year.	They are all nice but ... well, wait ...
	Hmm, it's expensive, but ...
	I don't know what I want.
	You decide first.
	Maybe next year.
	I need a little time.
	Maybe this, or maybe that, or maybe ...

2 The students express their opinion about four common decisions. Once they have filled in the grid, they can discuss the answers with their partner. Encourage them to use the phrases in the box. No answer key here (and for exercise 3) as the answers are subjective.

3 **Key verb: decide.** The students decide whether the statements are true or false for them. They can discuss their answers in small groups.

4 A matching exercise with more practice of *to decide* and also *to choose*.

1 B 2 F 3 A 4 C 5 E 6 D

5 Have students look at the grammar box on page 66 before matching the sentence halves.

1 C 2 E 3 A 4 B 5 D

Use **photocopiable 13** to get your students to use the structure *good/terrible/brilliant at doing something*.

- Make enough copies so each student can have one card. (There are eight per sheet.)
- Explain to your students that they are going to find out some of the talents of the other members of the group. They will each get a card and should ask questions to find someone who is, for example, *good at* fishing. Encourage them not to be too modest since everybody is good at something.
- It is a good idea to model the structure before they start:
  Teacher: *Jasmine, are you good at fishing?*
  Jasmine: *Me? No, I'm terrible at fishing.*
  Teacher: *How about you, Jenny? Are you good at fishing?*
  Jenny: *Oh yes. I'm fantastic at fishing.*
- Tell the students they should write the names of the students who are good at the various things on their card.
- After the activity, ask a few people for the most interesting things they found out.

6 Everyone or no one? The students will almost certainly need to look at the grammar box before they do this exercise on *everyone, no one, someone* and *anyone*.

1 anybody
2 everybody
3 Somebody
4 someone
5 everyone
6 nobody

7 Students see how much they know about their classmates. They then mingle and check.

8 2.2 Before listening, the students discuss how the things on the list normally change. They should discuss the answers with their classmates before listening.

Man	positive change: changed his job, from being a teacher to being a computer salesman. Negative change: Tom doesn't like changes at home (such as people moving the television).
Woman	decided to have children and stopped work, changed her hair from long and natural to short and business-like. She likes change.

9 **And finally ...** The students complete sentences about changes in their own life. Below are some suggested answers.

1 ... I first heard Tokio Hotel's first album.
2 ... I started learning English at evening school.
3 ... only eat healthy food.
4 ... I didn't have enough money for the petrol!
5 ... it is so expensive.

B I'm feeling lucky!

coursebook pages 68–69

1 Your students look at five photographs and decide why it might a lucky day for the people depicted. There are no definitive answers and hopefully your students will come up with some creative answers. Below are some suggested answers. (You might want to take this opportunity to point out the difference between *happy* and *lucky*, as both mean *glücklich* in German.)

1 His doctor told him that he doesn't need an operation.
2 They won a cruise in the Caribbean.
3 His dog found a gold watch.
4 They won a meal in a restaurant in a newspaper competition.
5 They won £50,000 on the lottery.

2 The students can complete the sentences about knowing when you are lucky. Again, there are no specific answers but here are some suggestions.

1 can help you find a job/who think your jokes are funny.
2 score a goal/win.
3 meet the man/woman of your dreams.
4 have a friend who has the solution.

In the second part of the exercise, the students tell their classmates about situations in which they have been lucky. You can encourage the others to respond using the phrases in the box.

3 Reading comprehension. Before reading, the students should look at the pictures and discuss what the story might be about. You might want to pre-teach *thunderstorm, lightning, electric current, to be burnt, to earth*. After reading you can get them to close their books and tell you the story because you've 'forgotten'.

4 The students match up expressions that appear in the text. If they're having problems they can look in the text.

boyfriend	find help
electric current	headphones
lucky escape	thunderstorms

5 The students read the statements and then discuss in small groups whether they think the person is lucky or unlucky. No answer key as they will make up their own minds.

6 2.3 Listening comprehension. Your students will listen to Mary's story. Before you play the recording, get them to read the statements and help with any unknown vocabulary. While they are listening, they can decide whether the statements are true or false.

1 True.
2 False. A wild cat attacked a girl called Alison.
3 True.
4 False. The cougar attacked Alison twice.
5 False.
6 False. But she thought the girl would die.
7 False. A teacher came with a group of boys.
8 False. She wore a face mask for a year.

Whether Alison can be considered lucky is a matter for debate – and hopefully your students will discuss freely.

7 A little exercise in which the students have to choose between *what to do* and *how to*. Pre-teach before having the students do the exercise.

1 how to	4 how to
2 how to	5 what to do
3 what to do	6 how to

When they have done the exercises, the faster students can add some more of their own. Once everyone has completed the exercise, they can ask each other the questions.

8 Looking at the negative form of some adjectives. Your students can read the blue box about making negative adjectives before they do the exercise.

1 unhappy	5 impossible
2 unhealthy	6 unprofessional
3 illegal	7 unfriendly
4 untrue	8 unsafe

Use this **photocopiable 14** to allow your students to practise negative adjectives.

- Make a copy and cut up the cards, keeping the sentences and the adjectives separate.
- Give the sentences to one half of your class and ask them to think what word comes at the end of the sentence.
- Give the negative adjectives to the other half of the class and ask them to think of sentences in which they could use those words.
- Then ask the students with the sentence to read out their sentences without saying the word. They can say 'Bong' instead. For example: *I want to fly like a bird but I can't because it is 'bong'*. The other students have to guess what 'bong' is.
- Alternative 1: Total anarchy as your students run around trying to match up the sentences and negative adjectives by reading them (not showing them) to each other.
- Alternative 2: Gentle version. Your students read out the sentences and decide how many of the negative adjectives could possibly fit the sentence. There can be more than one possibility.

9 **And finally ...** your students discuss the things they learnt at school, what their parents taught them and what they taught themselves to do. Hopefully they will come up with some nice stories. You may like to think of a few of your own to get the ball rolling.

C You win some, you lose some

coursebook pages 70–71

1 Your students discuss whether they normally find or lose a variety of objects. They should do this in small groups.

2 The students share their personal experiences of things they have lost and found. There should be some very interesting answers here! They should work in pairs initially and then share those stories with the group.

3 An interesting reading comprehension with some gaps that the students need to fill using the words in the box. Make sure they understand that there are two words per two-word gap.

1 taking/selling	4 happy/help	7 realized/contacted
2 took/police	5 enjoying/sights	
3 know/did	6 went/toilet	

In the second part of the exercise the students read the short phrases and decide who they think might have said them. There is some healthy room for debate but here are some suggested answers:

John: 1, 6, 7, 8 Shahla: 2, 4, 9 Shahla's husband: 3, 5

4 A short writing exercise in which the students choose a title of the story, and add two more sentences to the end of the story. No definitive answer here.

Extension activity: Your students can write a simple dialogue between either Shahla and her husband, or between John and a police officer. Help them with their writing but get them to keep it as simple as possible. It would be great if some students could act out their dialogue in a little role-play.

5 In pairs, the students discuss what they carry in their wallet or purse. This is a vocabulary boosting exercise and preparation for the listening comprehension in exercise 6. Note in American English a *driving licence* is called a *driver's license*.

6 **2.4** Listening comprehension in which the students will hear about an experiment a psychologist did with some wallets. Have the students read the three questions before they listen. You may need to play the recording more than once for them to get all the data.

240

a photo, a library card, lottery tickets

smiling baby photo 88%; puppy photo 53%; family photo 48%; photo of old couple, 28%; no photo, 1 in 7.

7 A reading exercise about the talented Levi Roots. The students have to match up the questions with Levi's answers.

Can you tell me about your sauce ... ?	1
How much did your home cost?	4
Did winning the £50,000 make you happy?	3
How poor were you?	2
What is the secret of winning in the world of business?	5
How much is your Reggae Sauce company worth now?	6

8 The students boost their vocabulary with a word search activity.

1 chief executive
2 to own
3 to rent
4 to take a chance
5 what it is worth
6 the othe day

9 **And finally ...** The students discuss things they've won. This could be a prize in a lottery, a prize at school, or perhaps even the Nobel Peace Prize!

8

At the end of unit 8 your students should:

- have talked about food and cooking.
- have practised the modals *can*, *can't* and *to be able to* and discussed their abilities.
- have discussed their shopping habits.
- know a variety of shops and what can be bought there.
- have practised the structure *Have you got ...?*
- have talked about restaurants and practised restaurant dialogues.

A Can you cook?

coursebook pages 74–75

1 The students look at the photographs of food and then look for a suitable phrase to go with them. There are no definitive answers as the students will have their own views on food.

In the second part of the exercise they discuss their favourite meal of the day and also things that they don't eat. You may need to help them with some of the vocabulary.

2 **2.6** Your students will hear a number of people being asked about who cooks at home. Give them time to read the sentences before you play the recording.

1 A 2 D 3 B 4 C

3 After looking at the language box which introduces *can*, *can't* and *to be able to*, you can have the students do the short exercise with a partner. They come up with their own answers so the answers below are just suggestions.

1 read and write
2 love
3 send a text message
4 juggle with five balls

4 The students can have some fun with a quiz about their cooking abilities (and get a lot of practice of using *can*). They should work in pairs and ask each other the questions. The person answering the questions first should listen to them rather than just reading them him/herself.

5 A personalization activity in which the students work with a partner and construct simple sentences using *can* and *can't*. Give them time to ask each other the questions before the feedback session.

Use **photocopiable 15** to give your students some more practice using *can*.

- There are eight cards on the sheet. Make enough copies so that each student has one card, and cut out the cards. Explain to the students that you want to find out about their abilities.
- Hand out the cards. Each student should ask as many other students as possible about the ability on the card. Encourage the students to use the phrase from unit 7. *Oh yes, I'm brilliant at ... / No, I'm terrible at ...*
- The person with the card then decides which category to put the person in. (They have three options.)
- In the feedback session it might be nice to hear some people who can sing like angels, watch people who can juggle with three balls, etc – but of course the main idea is to get them to use *can* in a natural way.

6 Reading comprehension. Your students read a text about a film called 'Julie and Julia' and complete the text with the phrases in the box.

1 and complicated at the same time
2 that's Meryl Streep in the film
3 just after the terrorist attack on 9/11
4 that's over 500 of them
5 only for a few days

In the second part of the exercise, the students have to decide whether it was Julie or Julia who did various things.

1 Julia
2 Julie
3 Julie
4 Julie and Julia
5 Julia
6 Julie
7 Julie

7 The students look at some basic recipes. (You may need to help them with the pronunciation: the word *receipt* is frequently used (wrongly) for *recipe*.) They can decide in groups what ingredients should go in, on and with the various dishes. There is plenty of room for healthy debate so no answer key here.

8 **And finally ...** The students answer the questions in small groups. If your students are competitive, you could have the different groups compete to get the most correct answers within a given time limit.

B Shops & shopping

coursebook pages 76–77

1 Your students match up a number of products with the shops in which they can buy them. They may not know the names of the shops so they may need some help here, though there are some clues in the pictures.

watches, rings and earrings	jeweller's
bread and cakes	bakery
medicine, soap and things for the bathroom	chemist's
trousers and T-shirts	clothes shop
boots and shoes	shoe shop
meat	butcher's
newspapers, magazines and cigarettes	newsagent's

2 The students match up signs with different places where you can go shopping. They should not limit themselves to the shops in the illustrations. Note that the term 'buy one get one free' forms the acronym BOGOF – which sounds like, but isn't, an insult. The term bogof is now quite well known in Britain.

Suggested answers:

organic	baker, butcher's
everything is fresh	bakery
visit our online shop	jeweller's, clothes shop
top quality	clothes shop
great reductions	shoe shop, clothes shop
10 for £1	bakery, chemist's
fantastic choice of goods	chemist's
everything you need	department store
designer brands	clothes shop, shoe shop
buy one get one free	chemist's, bakery

3 **2.7** Listening comprehension. The students will hear Jack and Zeynap talking about the tings they've bought recently. The students have to decide which shops they visited.

Jack	bakery, shoe shop, chemist's, hairdresser
Zeynap	chemist's, newsagent, clothes shop, butcher

4 A nice little discussion about the way your students shop. They should answer the questions in small groups before a larger feedback session.

5 What's true for you? The students say whether the statements are true for them. Then they can discuss the various statements with their partners.

6 Asking and answering questions. The students complete the questions in any way they like and then ask their partners. They could also write two more questions to find out about their partner's shopping.

7 **Quick quiz.** Students guess which department store the sentences describe: Harrods in London or KaDeWe in Berlin. Here the emphasis is on discussion, not on getting everything right.

The following facts are about KaDeWe:

(1) opening at 10 am
(5) opened in 1907
(6) bombed during WWII
(8) extra floor added
(11) lovely winter garden

8 Read through the grammar box on *Have you got ...?* with the students before having them match up the phrases and the shops in which they might be heard. Note that Americans tend to use *Do you have?* rather than *Have you got?*

1 B 2 F 3 D 4 C 5 A 6 E

Use **photocopiable 16** to give your students some practice with *have* got.

- Make enough photocopies so that there is one card for each group of 4–5 students. (Ideally you want four groups but you may have to be flexible depending on the numbers of students in your class.)
- Arrange your students into groups and choose one captain for each team. That person should be someone with a bag (or rucksack). Each team writes down its letter (A, B, etc) at the top of their card (or can give itself a name).
- Explain that the idea is to try to guess what a team captain from another team has in his/her bag. Make sure each group is guessing about a different team captain, i.e., Team A guesses about the captain of B, Team B about the captain of C, etc. Each team writes the name of the team captain they'll be guessing about on their card.
- Give the teams two minutes to discuss and write down 10 objects on their cards.
- While they are working, draw a table on the board for keeping score.

	A	B	C	D
Points				

- When the two minutes are up, explain how the scoring works. There will be three rounds (though if time is a problem you can reduce this to two) and each correct guess gets a point. If there is no clear winner, the game continues until there is one.
- Then start the game. Someone from team A asks the captain of team B: *Have you got keys (or a pen or a wallet, etc.) in your bag?* If the answer is yes, team A gets a point. The game continues around with each group asking about a different team's captain, like this:
  1 Team A asks B, B asks C, C asks D, D asks A (end of round one).
  2 A asks B, B asks C, C asks D, D asks A (end of round two).
  3 A asks B, B asks C, C asks D, D asks A (end of round three).
- An important rule, and one that makes the game more challenging, is that the students cannot ask about any object that has been mentioned before. If they do, they don't get the point.
- This is a fun game and good for practising common items and also lots of *Have you got ...?* questions. If you're American, or your students prefer American English, you may like to have the students ask: *Do you have a ... in your bag?* instead.

9 Explain the difference between *a pair of* and *a couple of*, then have the students complete the sentences.

1 couple
2 pair
3 pair
4 couple

10 **And finally ...** A prioritizing exercise in which students decide what is important for them when they go shopping. They should debate this with their partners and then in small groups. No answer key as they can make up their own minds

C Eating in or eating out?

coursebook pages 78–79

1 Your students discuss different food terms. There are no definitive answers so there is no answer key. The objective is to get the students to discuss the terms, and become familiar with all the vocabulary.

2 Here the students debate the positive and negative aspects of eating out. They should make notes during their discussion so that they can share the information with the whole group. The ideas in the boxes can help guide the discussion.

3 A reading comprehension and gapfill about going out to eat. The students can then debate which restaurants in the text can be found locally.

1 normal	5 different	9 fresh
2 boring	6 international	10 home-cooked
3 good	7 endless	
4 new	8 quality	

4 The students look at the restaurants in the photos and try to work out what is special about them. Note that the three restaurants are the focus of exercise 5.

5 A reading comprehension about the three restaurants above. Students complete the gaps in the table and finish the sentences. Suggestions for the latter below:

The Snow Hotel	Finland	It's cold because it's made of ice and snow.
Ithaa	Maldives	You eat under water.
Fortezza Medicea	Italy	The guards check your passport. The knives are plastic. The cooks are prisoners.

6 A vocabulary boosting exercise based on the text about hotels.

1 ceiling   2 prison   3 guards   4 knives

Extension activity: Get your students to talk about restaurants in their town and anything that is special about them. They can make a few notes about them (with some help from you). Then, in turn, they read out their notes and the other students try to decide which restaurant is being described.

7 **2.8** A listening comprehension about why people start a restaurant. Before they listen to the recording, your students should read the statements and decide whether they think they are true or false. When they listen they can check their answers.

1 T   2 F   3 F   4 T   5 T   6 T   7 F

8 In the first part of this exercise, the students decide whether the phrases are likely to be spoken by a waiter or a customer.

1 W   2 C   3 W   4 C   5 W   6 C   7 C   8 W   9 C   10 C

In the second part of the exercise, the students add some of the lines of dialogue to the three conversations.

A: 6, 3, 2   B: 5, 8   C: 4, 9

9 **And finally ...** The students tell each other about the last time they went to a restaurant. There are some questions to guide them, but they should feel free to ask any other questions they want to.

Journal II

See notes in the teaching tips (page 10) on ways to use the material in the journals.

Coursebook pages 82–89

Wait a minute, Mr Postman ...

Before reading

- Your students get into groups and discuss how often they send parcels (or even letters!) to or from foreign countries. How easy is it? How difficult is it?

After reading

- **Problems:** The students discuss in which country Lisa had the fewest problems - and in which country she had the most!

Disappearing Shopfronts of New York City

Before reading

- The students discuss favourite small shops in their own town. What do they like about them?

After reading

- **My favourite shop:** In groups, the students pick their favourite shop from the photo series and write a list of things which they can buy in that shop. Which group can produce the longest list?

Lost & Found

Before reading

- Get your students to discuss things which they have lost or found. Who has the most interesting story?

After reading

- **I've lost my voice:** The students choose three long words from the text. In turn, they mouth the words to their group, but don't say the word out loud. Can the other students see which word they are 'saying'?

- **Miming:** They students search the text for items that have been lost in London. They then do a mime to show what the object is. The other students have to guess what the object is.

City Break: Buenos Aires

Before reading

- Get your students to discuss what they know about Buenos Aires and what they would like to know about Buenos Aires. While they are reading they can check to confirm their ideas, or, hopefully, get the answers to some of their questions.

After reading

- **Three things:** In groups, the students discuss three things that they would like to do in Buenos Aires. They can then share their ideas with other groups.

- **In my country:** The students discuss the differences between their own town or city and Buenos Aires. For example. *In Buenos Aires, people eat at ten in the evening. In Switzerland, most people are in bed at 10 pm!*

Pretty in pink

Before reading

- Get your students to discuss what they would think if they saw a boy or a man in a pink shirt. What about a girl or a woman in a blue shirt?

After reading

- **Good or bad:** The students can discuss whether what Janice did was a good or a bad idea.

- **What colours mean:** They can discuss the range of colours and the associations we make with them. For example: red = danger.

9

At the end of unit 9 your students should:

- be able to talk about activities at work.
- be able to express preferences.
- be able to use the present continuous in a variety of situations.
- have practised expressions with *give*.
- be able to use state verbs to express opinions and *should* to give advice.
- can compare things using *more*, *less* and *fewer*
- have practised prepositions of place.

A What are you doing?

coursebook pages 90–91

1 Your students discuss a variety of situations and decide which they prefer. They can discuss this with their partner or in small groups. There is a small language box at the bottom of the exercise which they may find useful.

2 Exercise 2 is based on the four photos of offices and allows your students to practise their superlatives. They should remember that longer adjectives (usually) take *the most ...* form, while shorter adjectives take *the ....est* form. Ask the students how expensive it would be to rent each office. Once you have four prices, you can elicit *more expensive* and *most expensive* from them. Similarly, *cheaper* and *cheapest*.

3 A nice text about preferences to which the students have to add the missing phrases. This is to encourage your students to think in chunks rather than in individual words. Once the students have completed the text, don't forget to ask them their opinions. Do they agree or disagree with the text?

1 hate every minute
2 match how you feel
3 lie in bed for hours
4 depend on age or sex
5 say why some people
6 prefer wine to beer
7 prefer classical music to rock
8 work in an office
9 enjoy meeting people
10 go to work

4 A personalization exercise on preferences with a useful language box. Students give their own opinions here and share them with their group.

Use **photocopiable 17** to give your students practice expressing their preferences.

- Make enough copies so that each person in the group has at least one picture (there are twelve on the sheet). Cut out the pictures.
- Explain to your students that they are going to carry out a survey. The magic question is: *Which do you prefer?*
- Hand out the pictures to your students and have them move around the room asking their question, e.g. *Which do you prefer, chocolate or apples?* and collecting their classmates' responses.
- During the feedback session you can ask some of them for their survey results. For example: *Ten people prefer apples to chocolate. Four people prefer walking in the mountains to lying on the beach*, etc. What's the most surprising result?

5 **2.10** Listening comprehension with a nice introduction to the present continuous. Your students listen to a conversation and identify what the speakers and two of their colleagues are doing at the moment.

Matt is driving to a meeting.
Sonia is looking at the information about the programme.
James is standing right here and organizing the accommodation.
Steve is sitting at his desk and writing some emails. (He's not talking on the phone.)

6 A simple exercise to raise awareness of the difference between the simple present and the present continuous. Students have to decide whether the statement is talking about *now* (N) or some *general information* (G). If your students ask for the name of this new tense, you can give it to them, but the important part is that they are able to distinguish between the two forms.

1 G 2 N 3 G 4 N 5 G 6 N 7 G 8 N

7 A personalizing exercise in which the students change the sentences so that they are true for them. They also get lots of practice of the present continuous.

8 **And finally ...** The students match up the activities with the jobs. They may have different answers so the answers below are just suggestions. The important thing is for them to debate the possibilities with their partners.

A making decisions
B working with people
C using your hands
D making telephone calls
E (open answer)

B Things are different now

coursebook pages 92–93

1 A nice warm-up activity in which your students review the present continuous and do a class survey. Get them to work together so that they discuss the answers. You may like to contrast the present continuous with the simple present: T: *What's Jenny wearing today?* S: *She's wearing black jeans.* T: *Does she wear black jeans every week?* S: *No, sometimes she wears blue jeans.* T: *But at the moment ...* S: *... she's wearing black jeans.*

2 The students read the phrases in the boxes and then look at the photos. Can they see some of the activities? There is no answer key as there should be some debate as to the activities going on in the photos. Hopefully, your students will be using the present continuous.

> **Extension activity:** Get two students to look out of the classroom window and tell the others what is happening: *Any exciting action out there?* Ask for details about people's clothes, and what exactly they are doing. After a couple of minutes, ask them to sit down again, and you have 'forgotten' all the information. T: *There was something about a woman ...* S: *Yes, The woman with blonde hair is wearing a red coat.* T: *Oh yes, thank you. And is she smoking a cigar?* S: *No, she isn't. The man with the black hat is smoking a cigar.*

3 **2.11** A sounds good exercise in which students listen out for certain sounds. Note that the speaker in number 8 pronounces 'Do you' as 'Djew', which is a common contraction.

Key:

1 C	4 B
2 B	5 A
3 A	6 B, C

4 A nice matching exercise based on giving advice with *should*. Read through the grammar box with your students before having them do the exercise.

Key: 1 C 2 G 3 F 4 B 5 D 6 E 7 A

You may like to get your students to use the word *should* in the replies that don't already have one. For example: *You should close the window.* instead of *Close the window.*

5 Your students choose one of the three situations and then move around the class asking for advice. They should note down the best answers – and the funniest!

6 **2.12** Listening comprehension. Your students will hear Tim and Kay talking about what makes a good boss. They should complete the notes below the photos.

make **good decisions** | **be a good** communicator
be a good **listener** | **not have** favourites
know when to say **NO**

They can then think of some more qualities a good boss should have and can share them with the group.

7 Your students choose one of the three statements (the one they feel most strongly about) and tell their partner why they feel the way they do. If there is time, they can discuss all three statements.

8 **Key verb: give.** Your students have to complete some sentences using words that collocate with *give*.

1 hand
2 moment
3 idea
4 lift
5 smile
6 advice
7 call

9 The students read statements about work, friends and holidays and decide which statement they agree with. They then debate the statements with their partner.

0 **And finally ...** Your students read a short email and discuss with their partner things that a friend should and shouldn't do in Germany.

Model answers:

1 You should visit Krefeld. It's a lovely city.
2 You should try some German beer.
3 You shouldn't eat only Bratwurst. There are other good things to eat.

C Feeling at home

coursebook pages 94–95

1 Your students consider two statements and say which they would prefer. They may like to use the phrases in the language box. The object here is to generate debate rather than coming up with a definitive answer.

2 Your students compare two workplaces in the illustration and say which one most resembles theirs and why. You may like to teach them the words: *mess*, *tidy* and *untidy*. They may ask you for more vocabulary though this is covered in exercise 3.

3 A vocabulary boosting exercise in which your students look for the various items in the illustration. You may need to help them with some of the words.

Picture on the left	Picture on the right	Both
a plastic bag	a waste-paper basket	a desk chair
a coffee cup	a mouse mat	a desk light
a laptop		some files
a framed photo		a keyboard
a pair of glasses		
a plant		
a shelf with books		

2.13 Listening comprehension. In the second part of the exercise, the students match up the two halves of the sentences about the woman's workplace. They will need to listen carefully and you may like to stop the recording occasionally to give them time to find the matching halves.

1 C 2 H 3 E 4 D 5 F 6 G 7 I 8 B 9 A

4 A simple true/false exercise about the woman's workplace – but also using lots of prepositions of place. Your students may say that the computer is 'on the right side'. In English we normally say *on the right* or *on the right hand side*.

1 False. They are all on the right.
2 False. It's on the right.
3 Might be true but not 100% sure because we can't see the whole room.
4 False. It's on the desk.
5 False. There is a framed photo in front of the plant.
6 False.
7 False. The keyboard is part of the laptop.

5 The students describe the room in which they are currently sitting. They should take it in turns with their partner. They have some useful expressions in the language box.

In the second part of the exercise, the students describe a room from their home to their partner. It is a good idea to get the people listening to draw a plan of their partner's room rather than just listen.

You can use **photocopiable 18** to give your students more practice of prepositions of place.

- Make enough copies so there is one copy between two students. Cut the copies in half.
- Arrange your students in pairs so that they are facing each other.
- Explain to the students that they need to work together to complete the drawing of Bob's bedroom. Pre-teach *ashtray* and *racket*.
- Student A asks Student B about the items which are missing from his/her picture. Student B explains (not shows) where the items are and Student A draws the items. Make sure the students ask *Where is ...?* for singular nouns and *Where are ... ?* for plural nouns.
- Once Student A has finished drawing, student B can start asking and drawing.
- It is very important that this is an oral exercise. They should not show the other person their picture until the very end.
- Some students will work faster than others. The fast ones can double check their answers: The students can tell each other exactly where they drew the missing items.

6 In this exercise your students match up halves of sentences which include opinion (or state) verbs. Have them look at the grammar box first. Someone may ask you about a sentence like: *I'm thinking of moving to England.* However, in this case, the verb *to think* is not being used to express an opinion. Compare it to: *I think Manchester United are brilliant* where the speaker is clearly expressing an opinion. You would not say: *I am thinking Manchester United are brilliant.*

1 B 2 E 3 F 4 C 5 A 6 D

In pairs the students can then debate which opinions they agree with and disagree with.

Extension activity: Get your students to write down all the state verbs they saw in the previous exercise (plus any others they may know). Then they should brainstorm to think of as many things that they can apply to each state verb. For example: *I understand Russian. I understand nuclear physics. I don't understand men.* etc.

7 An exercise to get your students to look at the difference between *fewer* and *less*. Note it is quite common to hear native speakers use *less* with countable nouns. The most famous example is in supermarkets where some checkouts are for *ten items* or *less*.
There's no answer key as the students can make their own minds up.

8 **And finally ...** The students discuss two objects in their home that are important to them. This not only practises prepositions but also personalizes the exercise.

10

At the end of unit 10 your students should:

- can say what they *would* or *wouldn't like* to do.
- have looked at problem pages and giving advice.
- have looked at the key verb *make*.
- have talked about relationships and feelings.
- know some basic colours.
- have talked about feelings with *-ing* and *-ed* adjectives.
- can use imperatives to give instructions.
- have talked about newspapers and the parts of a newspaper.
- have practised *someone else*, *anything else*, *nowhere else* etc.

A Making an impression

coursebook pages 98–99

1 Your students discuss which person out of the three they would like to meet and say why they would like to meet him or her. Your students should say *I would like to meet ...* rather than *I like to meet ...* .

When doing an exercise like this, make sure that it is the student doing the work, not you. There is a danger it could turn out as: T: *So, Dani, which of the three people would you like to meet?* Dani: *The boy.* T: *And why would you like to meet the boy?* Dani: *He's got sexy eyes.* In this example, teacher has used the target structure twice, and the student hasn't used it at all. Compare this to: T: *So, Dani. What do you think?* Dani: *I'd like to meet the boy.* T: *Really? Why?* Dani: *Because he's got sexy eyes.* In this exchange, Dani speaks more than the teacher and even uses the target structure in an exchange that sounds natural.

2 In this exercise the students debate the factors that influence us when we choose who we want to meet. Get them to go through their answers in small groups. Are there any surprises?

3 The students look at the phrases and decide whether they are used in a positive or negative context. The object here is debate rather than right or wrong answers.

4 Reading comprehension. Your students read a problem page letter – and the response. They can debate whether the advice is good or bad.
In the second part of the exercise, they have to say whether the statements are true, false, or if they don't know (O).

Key: 1 F 2 T 3 T 4 O 5 F 6 T 7 T 8 F

Use **photocopiable 19** to give your students some practice writing and giving advice.

- Make a copy (or copies) and cut out the problems cards. (There are 12 in all.)
- Explain that you have some friends who need help. You want your students to give them some advice.
- Hand out the cards, one or two per pair of students. Each pair works together to write a suitable response (or responses if they have two cards) on a separate piece of paper. Make sure they keep their responses short, otherwise the task could take too long. (In fact, you might want to hand out small blank cards for their responses.)
- Collect all the responses and all the problems and redistribute them, giving one half of the class the responses and the other half the questions. Can the students match them up?

5 Some good advice – and some useful practice of the **key verb *make***.

1 mistake	6 mess
2 noise	7 friends
3 sure	8 money
4 serious	9 decisions
5 phone	10 feel

6 **2.15** Listening comprehension. Your students will hear a conversation between Debra and Bob. Give them time to read the questions before you play the recording. You may like to play it more than once.

1 C 2 B 3 A 4 A

Extension activity: There are other famous people that Debra and Bob would like to meet. Ask your students if they heard which ones.

Bob Wayne Rooney, Angeline Jolie, Tolstoy
Debra Nelson Mandela, Steven Spielberg

7 The students discuss four things that they would like to do. Have them read through the grammar box before working in pairs.

8 **And finally ...** the students form *would you like?* questions to ask their partners. Encourage them to ask more questions – they don't have to limit themselves to the six suggestions.

B Believe it or not

coursebook pages 100–101

1 A fun warmer on colours and things people associate with them. Get the students to work in pairs or small groups. Do they always agree? Note that your quicker students can add more items to the categories.

Suggested answers:

black	magic, night, tea
blue	ocean, sky, water
green	market, light, tea, tree
orange	light, oranges
purple	aubergine
red	alarm, apple, light, tomatoes
yellow	banana, cab, light, submarine

2 A fun little exercise to show students a kind of trick while reviewing colours. They will probably agree it is surprisingly difficult.

3 A reading comprehension about tricks and optical illusions. Hopefully your students enjoy the amazing street paintings by Julian Beever.

Suggested answers:

1 A woman is sunbathing in a pool in the first painting. Two men are stuck in a well in the second.

2 It's hard to tell.

3 open answer

4 An odd one out to review some of the vocabulary in the text. Answers may vary but here are some suggestions.

1 crisis
2 potato (or 'mouse' if the category is things to eat!)
3 jewellery
4 to confuse
5 pavement

5 A simple exercise in which your students look at *-ing* and *-ed* adjectives. Explain the differences with the help of the grammar box before having students do the exercise.

1 surprised	4 boring
2 annoying	5 tired
3 shocking	6 interesting

Extension activity: Ask your students to draw simple pictures of faces showing an emotion. The other students in the group have to decide what emotion is illustrated. This is a fun way to practise the *-ed* adjective forms. It is likely that some of your students may use the *-ing* form (*He looks tiring*) so may need some extra help here.

6 In this exercise your students discuss what makes them feel frightened, and when they feel annoyed.

Model answers:

frightening	thunderstorms, dangerous drivers
annoying	when people don't queue, when politicians lie

7 **2.16** Listening comprehension. Your students will hear Zena tell Fred how to do a magic trick. The students have to put the pictures in order. More importantly, can they learn how to do the magic trick? You may have to pause the recording to give them time to find the correct picture.

1 B 2 F 3 C 4 D 5 E 6 A

8 A quick exercise on imperatives based on a description of the magic trick. The students don't need to hear the recording again to complete this exercise.

1 A 2 I 3 C 4 G 5 F 6 B 7 E 8 D 9 H

9 An exercise so that your students can practise using imperatives.

1 be quiet
2 Have fun
3 Hurry up
4 try some
5 Have a good journey
6 Don't forget
7 do it again
8 Don't worry

Use **photocopiable 20** to give your students some more practice of imperatives.

- Make a copy, cut out the eight pictures and stick them up around your classroom. (If you have a large class, you put up two sets of cards on opposite sides of the classroom and have students work in two groups.)
- Tell the students to stand up and look at the various pictures. What do they think the people are saying? They can work alone or in groups. Have them write down the text for the speech bubbles (on a separate piece of paper).
- In the feedback session you can ask for some of the suggestions they have for each illustration.

10 **And finally ...** The lesson ends with a debate in pairs or small groups, using the target structures but also allowing the students to express their opinions.

C In the news

coursebook pages 102–103

1 Your students match up the parts of a newspaper with the images.

1 celebrity news/gossip, adverts
2 puzzles
3 sports pages
4 headlines, international news
5 TV guide
6 weather forecast

The students then discuss what parts of a newspaper they read – and why. The phrases in the box can help them.

2 **2.17** In this listening comprehension, the students will hear Shaun and Daisy talking about which parts of a newspaper they read.

	Shaun	Daisy
horoscope		✓
politics		
gossip	✓	✓
TV Guide	✓	✓
sport	✓	✓
crossword		✓

3 **2.18** Your students look at two famous people and try to decide what offences they may have committed. They then listen to the recording to see if they were right.

Bill	drove his car without a licence, didn't stop at a stop sign
Axl	bit a security guard

They can discuss other famous people who have done good or bad things.

4 The students complete some sentences with *someone else*, *nothing else,* etc. Read through the grammar box with them before they do the exercise.

1 nothing else
2 nothing else
3 somewhere else
4 someone else
5 somewhere else
6 someone else
7 anything else
8 anything else
9 nothing else
10 nobody else

Extension activity: Get your students to work in groups of about 5–6. Ask them to write two of the phrases from exercise 4 on pieces of paper and put them in a bag in the middle. In turn, they take out one piece of paper and try to elicit the phrase from the other students. For example: *I live with my wife and ... .*

5 A reading comprehension and discussion about scams, which are explained in the blue box. Having read the short texts, we hope your students will have been warned about such scams – and not learnt a new money-making scheme! You can ask them about other scams that they are aware of. There are lots out there.

6 A simple vocabulary-boosting exercise based on the vocabulary in the short texts.

1 victim
2 transfer
3 criminals
4 financial worries
5 administration
6 congratulations

7 **And finally ...** The students discuss some aspects of current news, and then, for the final activity, they should be as creative as possible in inventing a story about themselves. Alternatively, you can get them to write stories about each other – though do ask them to write something nice!

11

At the end of unit 11 your students should:

- be able to talk about future plans with *going to*.
- have practised countable and uncountable nouns.
- be able to talk about extremes using *too* and *so*.
- have practised superlatives.
- have looked at adverbs, including sentence adverbs.
- have discussed immigration.
- have practised phrases to use when leaving and returning.
- have studied the key verb *come*.

A What are you going to do?

coursebook pages 106–107

1 Your students match up the four pictures with the four seasons.

spring: 4 summer: 3 autumn: 1 winter: 2 (it's the frozen door handle of a car)

2 A true/false exercise about weather and the seasons.

1 False. Many countries don't have four seasons.
2 True.
3 False. We associate green with spring and summer.

3 Another exercise on the weather, and a lead-in to the listening comprehension in exercise 4. This time the students have to label some illustrations.

left column	right column
rainy and cool	thunderstorms
partly cloudy with a chance of rain	snow
windy	icy
partly sunny and warm	foggy

Extension activity: Can the students discuss today's or yesterday's weather? You could bring in a weather map from an old newspaper and use it to practise the vocabulary above.

4 2.20 Your students listen to two friends talking about their plans for the weekend and, in particular, the weather. They then complete some sentences about the weather 'today' and 'tomorrow'. Note that they are introduced to the *going to* future in the second group of sentences. More work will be done with this structure in exercises 5 and 6.

This morning	cloudy, but warm in the sun (according to Paul) foggy (according to Candy)
This afternoon	cloudy, but warm in the sun (according to Paul) lovely (according to Candy)
Tomorrow morning	rain
Tomorrow afternoon	windy
Tomorrow evening	thunderstorms

5 **2.20** A second exercise on the listening, this time with a focus on future plans.

1 the weather
2 rain
3 going to
4 going to sell

6 Another *going to* exercise in which your students have to match up the two parts. Before doing this exercise you may like to give some examples of *going to*: T (picking up a key): *What am I going to do?* S: *You're going to lock the door.* T (taking a piece of chalk or a marker): *What am I going to do?* S: *You're going to write on the board.*

1 B 2 C 3 F 4 A 5 E 6 D

In the second part of the exercise, the students ask and answer questions.

Photocopiable 21 will give your students some more practice with *going to*.

- Make a copy and cut it in half down the middle. Then cut out the individual question and answer cards.
- Give the question cards to one half of your class and the answer cards to the other half. Explain that this is an oral exercise and that they should speak to each other, not read each other's cards.
- Students mingle and try to match up the cards. Once they have, they can sit down.
- Alternative version: Before they start looking for the matching cards, the students could look at the card they have and speculate on what either the answer or question could be. It is interesting to see how accurate their guesses are.

7 Asking about the quality of things using *What is/was ... like?* Your students have to add the missing phrase to the sentences. A common mistake for some students in answer to the question *What's your husband like?* is to answer *Yes, I like my husband.* Explain that *like* in this context does not mean to 'find somebody or something pleasant'.

1 the weather
2 the food
3 the hotel
4 your teacher
5 your new job
6 the film

The students then get the opportunity to ask each other three questions about their partner's last holiday using the *What was/were ... like?* construction.

8 A quick look at countable and uncountable nouns. The students simply have to identify countable and uncountable nouns in the sentences. Read through the grammar box with them first. They may be surprised that words that are countable in one language may be uncountable in another, for example: *information*, *hair*.

	Countable	Uncountable
1	bank	money
2	books	time
3	friend	rice
4	vegetarian	meat
5	hotel	information
6	car	money
7	sports	football
8	holiday	fun

9 **And finally ...** the students debate some serious issues about the future. Don't forget you are there to help them with their English, not change their views on politics or the environment!

B Around the world

coursebook pages 108–109

1 A **quick quiz** to get your students thinking about places around the world. They shouldn't be expected to know the answers but may like to discuss some possibilities.

1	the smallest continent	Australasia
2	the biggest island	Greenland (though some say Australia)
3	the largest desert	The Sahara or Antarctica (see exercise 4)
4	most densely populated city	Manila in the Philippines (43,079 people per square kilometre)
5	oldest city	Damascus
6	least densely populated country	Greenland

2 The student read short texts about four cities and try to match them to the photos.

1 Zurich   2 Athens   3 Copenhagen   4 Milan

3 The students describe a city to their partners who have to try and guess which city they are talking about. You may like to model the activity before the students begin.

4 **2.21** Listening comprehension. Your students will hear Nina and Matt talking about the 'National Geographic' and travel. They have to listen for the order in which some things are mentioned.

1 a magazine
2 a desert outside Africa
3 a desert in Africa
4 people who do experiments
4 day and night
5 a TV presenter
6 moments in history

In the second part of the exercise, the students answer some questions based on the listening. Play the recording again so that they can listen out for the answers.

1 She likes the photos.
2 Because Antarctica is the coldest, the windiest and the highest continent.
3 Places that get very little rain.
4 Because nobody lives there.
5 Hemingway adventure.

Extension activity: Get your students to discuss where in the world they would like to go and take pictures for 'National Geographic'. Hopefully the others will be curious enough to ask the question: *Why?*

5 The students read about use of the word *too*, then do the matching exercise.

1 B 2 F 3 C 4 H 5 D 6 A 7 E 8 G

Use **photocopiable 22** to practise the use of *too* in an amusing way.

- Make a copy and cut out the cards, keeping the sentence beginnings and endings in separate piles.
- Explain to your students that your teaching assistant accidentally cut some great sentences in half. You need their help to put them back together.
- Half the class should take one 'beginning' card each and the other half of the class should take one 'ending' card each.
- The students then walk around and try to find the other half of their sentence. Make sure they read the cards to each other, not just show them.
- If they don't like their card - or can't find their partner, they are welcome to exchange their card for a new one, but should only have one card at a time.
- Alternative version for students who prefer things a little slower: Give a complete set of cards (cut out) to groups of 2–3 students. They have to match them up on the desk.

6 A longer reading exercise about Michael Palin (from Monty Python) and his travels. The students have to put his journeys in the right sequence. Below shows both the order in which they are mentioned in the text and the actual publication date of the corresponding book.

1 Around the World in 80 Days (1989)
2 Pole to Pole (1992)
3 New Europe (2007)
4 Full Circle (1997)
5 Himalayas (2004)
6 Hemingway Adventure (1999)

7 A vocabulary-boosting activity in which the students underline adverbs in the text about Michael Palin.

quickly, nearly, locally, dangerously

8 A straightforward gapfill on adjectives and adverbs. Have students read the grammar box first (and the information on page 138, if necessary) before doing the exercise.

1 carefully
2 quickly, slowly
3 comfortable
4 careful, calmly
5 perfectly
6 heavy

9 **And finally ...** The students read some sentences and decide which ones are true for them or are sentiments that they endorse. They should discuss the answers with their partners.

C I'm not from here originally ... coursebook pages 110–111

1 Your students discuss things they miss and things they enjoy when they are away from home. They should do this in small groups before a feedback session with the whole group.

2 Some new phrases people say when they're leaving home or coming back. The students have to decide when they might hear the phrases.

Leaving	Returning
Take care.	I'm back.
Hurry back.	Wonderful to see you again.
See you later.	Come in.
Come again.	You look wonderful.
Good luck.	
Keep in touch.	

Extension activity: Get your students to role-play leaving and returning. As they leave the room they should say something appropriate to the class, who might also call out something. When they return (seconds later) they should exclaim something and should be welcomed appropriately by the class. This should only be done once or twice as there are only a few things you can say in this situation.

3 A reading comprehension about two people who left their countries and moved to England. The students should read the texts and fill in the table.

Sergei	music, politics
Aristides	the weather, language problems
Both	his family, food from home, doing something new
Neither	feeling sad, sport

4 The students discuss people who left their country to live and work in a new country.

5 **Key verb: come.** The students match up the two parts.

1 E 2 A 3 L 4 F 5 D/G 6 K 7 I 8 J 9 B 10 H 11 C 12 G/D

6 **2.22** Students listen to a number of callers on a radio phone-in, talking about living in a multicultural society, and say whether the statements are true or false.

1 F 2 F 3 F 4 T 5 T

They should then consider advantages that immigrants bring to a country.

Suggested answers:

1 an enthusiastic, young workforce
2 good restaurants
3 skills not available locally

7 A simple exercise to raise awareness of different sentence adverbs. Have students read through the grammar explanation before doing the exercise.

originally	how something started that is now different
basically	general comment
ideally	what would be perfect
luckily	a good situation
theoretically	what could possibly be true
unfortunately	something that we feel sorry about

They then do the exercise to the right of the grammar box: using adverbs from the previous exercise to complete the sentences.

1 Unfortunately,
2 Luckily,
3 Basically,
4 Theoretically,
5 Ideally,

8 **And finally ...** Students can work in pairs or small groups to tell each other about their homes and the origin of their belongings.

Journal III

See notes in the teaching tips (page 10) on ways to use the material in the journals.

Coursebook pages 114–121

My Airplane Facts ...

Before reading

- Your students get into groups and discuss some of the problems associated with flying economy class. After the discussion they can share their ideas with the group.

After reading

- **What about you?** How many of the things on Lisa's list have they experienced?
- **Seven problems:** There are seven problems. Students can work in groups to think of solutions to the problems Lisa mentions. They can share their best ideas with the class.

Faces of Tomorrow?

Before reading

- The students look at the two big photos on page 116 and 117 and discuss where these people might be from.

After reading

- **Which cities?** In groups, the students talk about the many cities that Mike has lived in. Has anyone been to those cities? Which ones would the group like to visit?
- **Word categories:** Can the groups find words to fit these categories: 'parts of the body', 'nationalities' and 'places to live'. How about 'adjectives' and 'adverbs'? Which group finds the most?

City Break: Melbourne

Before reading

- Get your students to discuss what they know about Melbourne and what they would like to know about Melbourne. While they are reading they can check to confirm their ideas, or, hopefully, get the answers to some of their questions.

After reading

- **Making plans:** The groups choose three things they would like to do in Melbourne. They can then compare notes with other groups.
- **Comparing cities:** As this is the last journal of A1, students may like to compare the cities in the three journals. Have them sit in groups of three, one looking at the Berlin text, one the Buenos Aires text and one the Melbourne text. How many similarities and differences can they find?

"If you have an idea – try it!"

Before reading

- Get your students to look at the pictures. What do they think the story will be about? (They might remember the story from Unit 5 Part C.)

After reading

- **Making money:** Kyle says, "If you have an idea, try it." Do the students have any good ideas for making money without working too hard?
- **Bartering:** Kyle talks about his attitude to money and to barter. Do your students agree with Kyle? Have they ever bartered something?

Mayor – have you put on weight?

Before reading

- Get your students to discuss whether they think the local politicians are paid too much, too little or about the right amount of money.

After reading

- **Good or bad:** In groups, the students discuss whether they think weighing the mayor is a good idea to monitor his or her income?

I could eat a horse!

Before reading

- The students can read the title and look at the photo. Then they can discuss what they think the story might be about. You could then explain what the expression *I could eat a horse* means: *Ich habe einen Bärenhunger*.

After reading

- **Just desserts:** In groups, the students can discuss whether Richard got what he deserved.

12

At the end of unit 12 your students should:

- have discussed different ways of communicating.
- have looked at the key verb: *keep*.
- have talked about body language.
- have looked at the irregular adverbs *well* and *badly*.

A Keep in touch

coursebook pages 122–123

1 Your students look at the four pictures and discuss the advantages and disadvantages of communicating in that way. Below are some suggested answers.

	advantages	disadvantages
flowers	they look and smell great, popular gifts	they are dead after a few days, some people are allergic to them
card	they can amuse people	It takes them days to arrive or they can get lost in the post
text message	instant, inexpensive	quite impersonal
note	quick, nice to have something written by hand	can get lost

In the final part of the exercise, they discuss other ways of communicating. (Some answers are provided in exercise 2.)

2 The students look at six short texts and fill the gaps there (there are three gaps per text) with a set of verbs from the list. (Note that the order of the verbs in each set is fixed and shouldn't be changed.)

Write letters.	receive | find | talking
Call often.	pick | need | knowing
Send cards.	show | choose | describes
Send someone a present!	make | show | getting
Email or chat online.	make | start | keep
Use Skype.	call | live | have

They then discuss which they do most often and which they find most difficult. This could develop into an interesting debate – for example about why men don't like long telephone conversations!

Use **photocopiable 23** to get your students to practise their writing skills.

- Make enough copies so that each student can have at least one card. (There are twelve cards per sheet.)
- Tell your students that you want them to write a short note (of 20–30 words) to a friend on a separate piece of paper that they can hand to you. Explain that it is very important that they don't tell anyone what they are writing. It is a secret note.
- While they are writing, you can walk around and offer help where needed.
- Once they have finished writing, collect the notes and put them into a bag.
- Redistribute the notes and see if the students can match them with the original instructions. (To help with this and to get students up and moving, you can stick the cards on the wall around the room.)
- If there are more than twelve students, then the students can compare the different notes that were written.

3 In the first part of the exercise, the students match up words in the box to make short phrases connected with communicating.

computer screen	video game	text message
electronic device	social life	

2.24 Then they listen to a conversation with a woman who is concerned about the effect of new technology on children. Give them time to read the opinions before you play the recording. They have to tick those that they hear. Note that they won't hear the exact words in the opinions, but the ideas. To help them, you can tell them there are 5 out of the 8 – and of course you can play the recording more than once.

They hear: 1, 4, 6, 7 and 8

Finally, they debate how much time people should spend doing various activities. Once they have discussed how much time they should spend, you might like to ask them how much time they actually *do* spend on those activities.

4 **Key verb: keep.** The students match up 12 utterances or mini dialogues, which all contain phrases with *keep*.

1 C 2 F 3 B 4 L 5 G 6 E 7 A 8 H 9 D 10 K 11 J 12 I

5 **And finally ...** Students then discuss what they use the internet for.

B Say what you mean

coursebook pages 124–125

1 Your students look at the photos of people showing a range of emotions. They debate how the people are feeling at the moment and use expressions from the language box to voice their opinion.

2 **2.25** The students listen to Kim Jenners, a psychologist, talking about body language. They have to listen carefully and fill in the information in the table. Before they listen, have them read though the list. Can they predict what the answers will be?

Key: man: 2, 5, 6, 7

woman: 1, 3, 4

After the listening, the students can try to replicate the positions of the man and the woman.

3 You may need to play the recording again for the students to get the answers in exercise 3. It may be interesting for your students to discuss what gestures they use to indicate these things before they listen to the psychologist again. Not all of the gestures match with the feelings so this exercise is to generate debate.

Key: Some suggested answers:

protection: 1, 6, 7
hesitation: 3
not being interested: 3
a sign of support: 5

Use **photocopiable 24** to do a light-hearted activity on body language and emotions with your students.

- Make enough copies so that each student has a card. (There are 16 cards per sheet so you will need to make more copies if you have a large class.)
- Students can work in small groups or as a class. (The former is better for more reserved students, the latter for a class of extroverts.)
- They take it turns to use body language and facial expressions to express the emotion or behaviour on the card while the rest of the group or class tries to guess what is being portrayed.
- Alternatively, if your class likes competitions, you can have students work in two teams and see which team makes the most right guesses.

4 Lots of expressions with *language*. Can you students work out what they mean?

Key:
1 sign language
2 the language of love
3 a dead language
4 first language
5 bad language
6 the official languages
7 body language

5 A reading text which the students have to put in order. In the answer key below, the first word of each section is given.

1 Communication ...
2 elements ...
3 Different ...
4 cultures ...
5 their fingers ...
6 they open ...
7 your stomach ...
8 head to show you ...

In the second part of the exercise, the students look at the gestures and discuss what they mean. Only three of them were mentioned in the text so students will have to guess or pool knowledge on the others.

Pictures in order from left to right:
Six, when counting (in Japan)
There's a bad smell.
Someone is drunk. (in France)
It's delicious. (in Italy)
You're late!/Hurry!

Extension activity: Get your students to brainstorm ideas about body language from around the world. After working in groups they can share the most interesting (and hopefully not too rude) examples that they heard. You may like to make a game of this. Allow the student to make the gesture and the other students have to guess what it means and which country it comes from.

6 Get your students to read the language box on *well* and *badly* before they do the exercise.

1 Well done
2 well equipped
3 well made
4 badly hurt
5 badly dressed
6 well off
7 well paid
8 well qualified

7 **And finally ...** Put your students in groups of 3–4. Give them some time to prepare a short 'dialogue' using only gestures. Can the other students guess what it means? Speaking of gestures, you might want to tell students that in the UK, two fingers (the index and middle finger) raised towards someone, is offensive. Many foreigners go into pubs in the UK and ask for two beers, raising two fingers to indicate how many beers they want, not realizing what this means to British people. Let's hope that after completing the book they will be able to order two beers, two cakes or two cups of tea *without* the need to lift their fingers!

Notes

Notes

Notes